LEGALIZE 'EM!

DENIS FEEHAN

IUNIVERSE, INC.
NEW YORK   BLOOMINGTON

LEGALIZE 'EM!

iUniverse books may be ordered through booksellers or by contacting:

iUniverse
1663 Liberty Drive
Bloomington, IN 47403
www.iuniverse.com
1-800-Authors (1-800-288-4677)

Because of the dynamic nature of the Internet, any Web addresses or links contained in this book may have changed since publication and may no longer be valid.

ISBN: 978-1-4502-4470-1 (sc)
ISBN: 978-1-4502-4471-8 (ebk)

Printed in the United States of America

iUniverse rev. date: 8/27/2010

INTRODUCTION

The war on drugs has been fought for more than a hundred years and it has been a colossal failure throughout that time span. That is because the American people (and just about every other country) want their drugs. We use Alcohol, Marijuana, Cocaine, Heroin and a whole heap of uppers and downers to keep ourselves medicated and recreated. That demand is insatiable and eternal. The misguided fight against the use of those drugs is futile and expensive. I am not condoning the use of drugs. I am simply arguing that the war on drugs in the United States is too expensive to American society, both in the criminals it creates and the cash it consumes. The only reasonable answer is to legalize it, regulate it and tax it as steeply as wine and whisky.

Legalization is not a new idea. It is not even a new experience for America. We will begin our discussion by revisiting the failed national policy of prohibiting the manufacture and sale of alcohol in this country, from which we have apparently learned nothing.

The 18th amendment to the U.S. Constitution, which forced alcohol underground, created a powerful monster in a semi-hidden cave. It built the Mafia into an organized and brutally violent enterprise. It placed underpaid Federal agents in the pathway to corruption. Quality control didn't just stop, it reversed itself. Producers intentionally diluted the alcohol they fed to consumers. That dilution produced dangerous, even fatal, results. And the citizens that it didn't kill had to pay a fortune for the administration of Prohibition. We eliminated most of those evils (the Mafia remains) simply by legalizing the manufacture and sale of alcohol.

We will note a parallel to these problems when we visit the cost of the war on drugs. The dominant parallel, the big dog of prohibiting anything that the public really wants, is money. Big fat stacks of U.S. greenbacks. The Mafia got the booze bucks and the drug lords get loads of loot for their cannabis and cocaine.

Those dollars, courtesy of our foolish drug war, have created criminal organizations all over the world - most notably the Columbian cartels and, more recently, the barbarous, murdering cartels that have brought anarchy to Mexico. Of particular concern to the citizens of the United States, the Mexican cartels have exported their violence to the U.S. along with their drugs.

Drug associated violence is not the sole purview of the Cartels, of course. Terrorists the world over have sold drugs routinely in order to finance their armies of suicide bombers. Closer to home, street gangs in every city have one thing in common - they all sell drugs. Some specialize in pimping, others in extortion, but every gang deals drugs. We can stop the Cartels and the terrorists and the gangs by simply taking away their lifeline - the sale of drugs.

Those drug selling gangs have also managed to corrupt government officials on both sides of the U.S./Mexican border. For the hapless Mexican policemen, it's a case of take the money or die. Worse yet, it's take the money or we'll kill your kids. And your wife and your parents. Some choice. For the U.S border agents, it's the opportunity to buy a houseboat on Havasu or park a corvette in their carport. All they have to do is look the other way when a truck full of weed enters into the States. Wouldn't be the first time and it won't be the last.

Also ongoing is the practice of diluting the drugs with various, often dangerous ingredients. Drug dealers, who are murderers, are generally comfortable breaking the FDA rules concerning consumer protections. This rule bending tendency of the drug lords is not necessarily a serious concern with marijuana but it is a big problem with the harder drugs. The unpredictability of the strength of a hit of heroin, for instance, has been responsible for fatal overdoses in most American cities.

Less dangerous but certainly more universally painful is the financial cost of the war on drugs. From the feds at the DEA down to the local beat cop, billions of our dollars are spent chasing a never-ending supply of drug dealers. When they do catch one, there is a cost to prosecute the druggies and, paradoxically, often a cost to defend them too. If the drug users are convicted, we spend thousands of dollars a year to incarcerate them. And that's for the healthy ones. The sick ones are really breaking the bank.

And spending money putting drug users in prison is only one side of the budgetary coin. Equally taxing to taxpayers is the loss of potential government revenue. If, for instance, tobacco companies were allowed to grow pot, legitimate jobs would be created on the farms. Those jobs would generate income taxes. The tobacco company profits would generate corporate taxes. Finally, every ounce of pot or gram of coke sold at the local liquor store would be taxed. As with alcohol, the drugs would be subject to a very hefty "sin tax."

But cash isn't the only concern with the legalization of drugs. There seems to be a fear in the general population that legalization would lead to a nation of addicts. To address that issue, we will look at a of couple examples of contemporary legal use - the coffee houses in Amsterdam and the medical marijuana stores in California.

But, before we get to those exotic locales, we are going to go back in the time machine to a gentler time, when baseball was the national pastime and speakeasies were the national good time. We will begin, as promised, with the U.S. prohibition of the manufacture and sales of alcohol. Interestingly, the *us*e of alcohol was not forbidden by the new law.

PROHIBITION

The Prohibition Era allows us a unique opportunity to view the overall effect of government intervention in the supply of a product which is in high demand. The Prohibition Era was not the only time in which authorities in the several states had sought to curtail the demand for alcohol. There were many previous, and often successful, localized attempts at "drying" up the country. However, *national* prohibition created problems that the local ordinances did not. Proponents of prohibition did not know what they were getting into when Congress passed the 18th amendment and its companion, the Volstead Act. Those two pieces of legislation, acting together, prohibited the manufacture and sale of alcohol but not, interestingly, its consumption.

That legislation led to an insatiable demand for alcohol that legal enterprises could no longer supply. Predictably, illegal enterprises began to fill that gap in supply. These "bootleggers" soon found that in order to survive, they needed to begin to act like the big business that they had actually already become. That need was filled by the emergence of the Mafia, with its centers in New York City and Chicago.

Once in business, the Mafia began to deal with a fundamental concept in business - competition. Legal businesses try to "kill" their competition by holding sales, increasing selection or building more stores. The Mafia literally killed its competition. Gang wars broke out all over the country, especially in New York and in Chicago, where the "Saint Valentine's Day Massacre" remains a prime example of the brutality of those wars. In response to the needless killing, a "Commission" was created by one "Lucky Luciano" to allow for a more businesslike method of settling disputes among the gangs.

In addition to countering the competition, the Mafia also had to contend with city hall. In order to stay out of jail, mobsters needed the cooperation of the local and federal authorities. That protection was easily bought by the mob. Mafia cash that should have been in the government's coffers, as tax revenue from the sale of the alcohol, found its way instead into the bank accounts of judges, federal agents and local beat cops.

Protections in place, the Mafia, like any good business, looked to increase profits wherever possible. Unfortunately for the drinking public, the criminal liquor salesmen did not have to report to any government agencies or abide by those agency's many restrictive consumer protections. This allowed the bootleggers to routinely "cut" the alcohol that they sold. They added wood alcohol and other liquids to the stock liquor in order to get two or three bottles of finished product where originally there had been only one. This adulteration of the liquor led to an inconsistent product potency which could, and did, cause blindness and even death to its consumers.

While prohibition physically harmed some American citizens, it had a severely negative impact on the wallets of the entire American population. The economic cost of prohibition was enormous. On one hand, Federal and State treasuries lost all of the tax revenues, both income and sales taxes, that it had collected prior to Prohibition. Likewise, those agencies lost the income taxes from the employees who continued to work in the new, illegal, alcohol "industry."

On the other hand, spending was *increased* dramatically. Federal and State agencies were created or beefed up to fight the good fight against booze. Courts were impacted with prohibition prosecutions and the jails and prisons were faced with additional prisoners for whom to provide food, clothing, health care and housing.

And the quality of life in America took a hit as well. The crime rate rose during Prohibition. Of course, it wasn't supposed to be that way. Elimination of the demon rum was supposed to make America a safer place to buy a house and raise a family. It did neither of those.

HISTORY

Prohibition of alcohol, at least in part, had been present in North America from almost the beginning of the European occupation of the continent. New York, Massachusetts and the Plymouth colony all restricted the use of alcohol as early as the 17th Century. In 1735, the first outright ban on alcohol was enacted in Georgia. These laws were generally failures.[1]

The 19th century saw a new fervor for prohibition, promoted in the most part by religious leaders of the time, such as Cotton Mather and Dr. Lyman Beecher. As a result of the work of these Christian anti-alcohol proponents, as well as other, secular adherents, the State of Maine passed an alcohol ban in 1851 that was the first of several successful succeeding bans. [2]

After the civil war, the movement began to gain momentum. Two organizations were at the vanguard of the fight. These were the Women's Christian Temperance Union (WCTU) and the Anti-Saloon League.

The WTCU was founded in 1874, in Cleveland, Ohio. It was chartered to work toward a ban on alcohol, tobacco and drugs. Frances E. Willard was an early leader of the WCTU. Under her leadership, the WCTU also became involved in Women's rights, specifically women's suffrage. The Anti-Saloon League was formed in 1895, amid a new round of prohibitionism. The Anti-Saloon League emphasized abstinence from alcohol as well as the eradication of the Saloon. A sympathetic adherent to that second precept was one Carry Nation.[3]

Carry Nation was an activist who took her work seriously. Hers was the cause of the saloon. She found a way to close them up: she chopped them down. Starting in Kiowa, Kansas, she used her walking stick and big rocks to break whatever was breakable in the bars. In Wichita, she began using her signature weapon, the hatchet. She also attacked bars in the capital city, Topeka. Carry Nation became a well known figure in the fight against liquor. She eventually traveled around the USA, Canada and Britain, spreading her message.[4]

By the turn of the 20th century, prohibition had become widespread. Early in its second decade, no later than 1913, so many anti-alcohol laws had been passed that half of the country was already covered by prohibition. To add to the umbrella which was slowly drying out the country, the Wartime Prohibition act was passed in 1918. This bill was meant to keep grains out of the distilleries and into the bakeries, where they could be used to make food for the troops going off to fight a completely unnecessary "Great War". All of these local laws created a country that was primed and ready for an all out ban. [5]

THE LAW

The 18th Amendment was passed by Congress on December 18, 1917. It was ratified by the several states on January 16, 1919 and took effect on January 17th, 1920. The Amendment stated that the "manufacture, sale or transportation of intoxicating liquors ... the importation thereof into, or the exportation thereof from the United States ... is hereby prohibited." Both the federal and state governments were given the power to enforce the Amendment.

To aid in that enforcement, Congress passed the Volstead Act. This act set the rules that related to the 18th Amendment. In addition to the manufacture and sale of alcohol, the act outlawed the advertisement of alcohol and the possession of any equipment that was needed for alcohol manufacturing.

The act also spelled out the penalties for violation. A first offense, for instance, was punishable by a fine of "not more than $1,000" and jail time "not exceeding six months". A second offense could cost from $200 to $2,000 and as much as five years in prison. However, it "shall not be unlawful to possess liquors in one's private dwelling … provided such liquors are for use only for the personal consumption of the owner." So you couldn't manufacture it, you couldn't transport it or sell it, but once you had it in your home, drink away me hearties!![6]

And drink they did, despite the 18th Amendment, ratified by the states and the Volstead Act passed by Congress. And, irregardless of the protestations of the Christian and secular "drys" who were certain that a new and better world was at hand, they drank and drank and drank some more.

SMUGGLING

But in order for the masses to keep drinking, a new mechanism was required. The legal distribution of liquor was no longer allowed. Not to worry. The criminals figured that out soon enough. They began to supply the ever present demand. They supplied that demand through small scale home production, which we will visit later, and through a much larger scale of international supply, smuggling.

Smuggling was a big time proposition. The illegal liquor came from many different locales where liquor was still legal: Canada, Europe, Mexico and the Caribbean.

In 1922, a writer for the New York Times observed that the land up north was a virtual Garden of Eden for bootleggers. And Detroit was their main target. Smuggling occurred on all of the borders of the United States, but the great state of Michigan was affected the worst of all. Three water routes, Lake St. Clair and both the Detroit River and the St. Clair River, entertained a running battle between bootleggers and government alcohol agents. The roads and rails of the northeast were equally crowded with suppliers of spirits as well as government agents who were attempting to slow the flow of illegal booze. Some 75 per cent of Prohibition-era liquor was smuggled in through the three waterways."[7]

The booze came over the border on boats, trucks, trains and airplanes. Citizens who worked in Detroit smuggled the spirits in their boots, coats, hot-water bottles and even in hollowed out eggs! Everyday people were making a few extra bucks everyday. One fisherman said that he could earn more cash on one run of booze than he could fishing on his boat all year."[8]

The really big bucks, though, were made by the criminals. They had the funds to facilitate large deliveries. They loaded boats, large and small, with shipments of liquor from Canadian docks. The local waterways were used to bring the goods to market in the states.

The criminals brought their goods to market on solid ground as well. The booze came across the border in cars and trucks. Not to be outdone by the auto industry, trains and airplanes were also loaded up with 80 proof for consumption in the United States. [9]

This enterprise was aided, with pleasure, by the Canadian distilleries. They were prohibited by law from shipping their goods to countries that prohibited alcohol. For all practical purposes, this meant the United States. However, the goods found their way to American glasses in a couple of different ways. First, we had smuggling. The distilleries had docks on the Canadian side of the waterways. Anyone could simply float a boat up to the dock and buy booze. Smugglers did that. Then they took their purchases to America.[10]

Second, the distilleries could legally ship their wares to any country that did *not* have national prohibition. That included Canada itself. Many Canadians ordered cases of booze for "personal consumption" and then smuggled the spirits to speakeasies in Detroit. Those with bigger plans - that would be the criminals - shipped liquor laden railroad cars to Mexico. That "destination", however, was only meant to put the authorities on the wrong track. Although the booze definitely chugged across the Canadian border, it generally derailed short of the Rio Grande. In addition to Mexico, other "official destinations" for alcoholic beverages that found their way south to the United States included Cuba and the Caribbean islands.[11]

But Cuba and the Caribbean islands were more than just fraudulent destinations for the southbound Canadian shipments of liquor. They were also frequently the *starting point* for spirits that were being sent northward to the United States. Ships from those locales would drop anchor in international waters, beyond the three mile limit, and service the rumrunners. Both professional bootleggers and folks who just wanted some personal use liquor bought from these merchants. Peter McWilliams noted that a whole slew of recreational boats were rented during the prohibition years - obviously just to buy offshore booze."[12]

A reporter for the New York Times wrote about just such a ship. A steamer, bound for Africa and loaded with liquor was missing 75,000 gallons from its ship's inventory when it was recounted by the authorities. Apparently, bootleggers had parked the large, alcohol laden ship off the shore of the U.S and used smaller boats to run the booze to the coastline.[13]

Not to be outdone, Mexico also became a staging spot for illegal alcohol destined for the United States. The border towns between the two countries did a big business moving the mixings for margaritas to the kitchens of the American southwest.[14]

THE MAFIA

Both the northern and southern borders of the United States were certainly problematic but here, in between the borders a powerful new problem was being born: The Mafia. Prior to Prohibition, the local gangsters were just that, local. It was every gang for himself. But the sheer size of the liquor business and the enormous profit in the business of selling prohibition liquor generated required a level of cooperation that did not previously exist. Like all businesses, organization was needed. Rules had to be written and followed. As there was plenty of money to go around, "sales territories" needed be assigned and adhered to. The emergence of the Mafia fit those needs.

Criminal gangs did not start with prohibition, of course. Prior to prohibition, street gangs already existed in America. For immigrants living in the Italian and Polish ghettos, for instance, many of whom were illiterate and did not speak English, joining a gang was one way to make a living. American born toughs who grew up in these neighborhoods also saw the gangs as an easy way to make a living. The local gangs that these goons joined paid these ne'er-do-wells to help run the various core pre-prohibition businesses of the gang - prostitution, numbers, extortion, theft, etc.

So as prohibition began, the gang lords and their minions were making money, but they were not making huge money. This was because they were not organized. Each gang was autonomous and each wanted as much of the local business as possible. As they were unable to advertise their businesses or run sales promotions to improve their personal percentage of that business, they routinely reverted to the "hostile takeover."

Although many "soldiers' lost their lives, a more common target of the hostile takeover was the leader of the gang. Being the leader of a gang was, therefore, a dangerous business. Capeci reported that being a boss could end your being at all. With their very lives on the line, gang leaders were more than willing to listen to a plan that would stop the killing. Enter "Lucky Luciano."[15]

Charles "Lucky" Luciano had a vision. He saw a world in which they all just "got along." He felt that there was enough money to go around without killing anyone. Mostly, the key was organization. The bad guys had to do business like the good guys. Business suits and lawyers could be more powerful than leather jackets and switchblades.[16]

Luciano's superior, Joe "the Boss" Masseria, was less the visionary. Again, think hostile takeover. So, although Luciano envisioned an organization in which a board of directors would make the rules and fighting would be kept to a minimum, a minimum amount of fighting would still be necessary. Not for the first time, Lucky Luciano helped a Mafia chieftain to his final burial place.[17]

Luciano's rise to the top was described by the FBI as the most important moment in the organization of organized crime. Luciano changed the previously scattered gangsters into a modern, corporate-like machine. The new Mafia focused on making money, not war. And, led by prohibition profits, the lowlifes were making top dollar.[18]

As Luciano had predicted, there was enough business for everybody. Fighting was usually unnecessary. The five families each got their own territory. The idea was that each family would stay within their own confines. However, disputes inevitably arose, sometimes ending in bloodshed. Luciano, the slick dressed, nouveau gangster, wanted to solve these disputes without warfare. To further that aim, he helped create The Commission, in 1931. This was a sort of board of directors that could solve disputes between families without the heretofore deadly violence. Sometimes they were able to keep the peace in New York and sometimes they voted to solve a problem by force. But they voted. [19]

But that was New York. Other cities were less sophisticated. In Chicago, for instance, Al "Scarface" Capone did not need votes. His vision of organized crime was Al Capone runs things and every one else stays out of his way. A well documented example of this management style was the attempted rubout of "Bugs" Moran in what became known as the "Saint Valentine's Day Massacre."

The Saint Valentine's Day Massacre was the polar opposite of Lucky Luciano's businessman's paradise. It was a prime example of kill or be killed. Zero cooperation. Al Capone wanted to run Chicago. Bugs Moran and his gang were in the way. Gee, what to do?[20]

This is pure speculation on my part, of course, because no one was ever convicted of the massacre, but Al Capone set the whole thing up. Capone recruited one Jack McGurn to set up the job and paid McGurn $10,000 plus expenses to pull it off[21].

McGurn brought in out-of-town gunmen so that local gangsters as well as the authorities would not know who they were. Also, there would be no obvious connection to Al Capone. From St. Louis, he brought in Fred "Killer" Burke. Burke's job was to head up the group. He would receive a cash payment of $5,000 for his management efforts. Next aboard was a gunman named James Ray. Third, for $1,000 each, Joseph Lolordo, John Scalise and Albert Anselmi joined the group. These were all well known gangsters. The latter two had been hired by the Capone temp agency several times before. McGurn also recruited two mobsters from the Purple Gang in Detroit. They were the Keywell brothers, Harry and Phil, and they were brought in as lookouts. In that capacity, the brothers took up residence at 2119 North Clark St, near the headquarters of "Bugs" Moran, a garage at 2122 North Clark St.[22]

The plan was ingenious. McGurn set up the massacre by having one of his hijackers sell a shipment of booze to "Bugs" Moran on the cheap. The second buy was set up on February 13th. The goods were to be delivered the next day, February 14th, 1929, St. Valentine's Day.[23]

McGurn dressed two of the thugs up as cops and two others in street clothes. He sent them to Moran's garage in a stolen police car. When the fake cops came into the garage, the seven men who were there ("Bugs" Moran had seen the police car and did not enter the garage), thought little of it. They expected that they were in the middle of some inconsequential shakedown. They complied with the order to drop their guns and line up against the wall. What happened next must have taken them completely by surprise. Capone's "cops" pulled out two machine guns, a rifle, and a pistol and started shooting. All seven went down. Six died there in the garage and the seventh died at the hospital, steadfastly refusing to name his assailants.[24]

After gunning down the seven men and leaving them in a pool of blood, the assassins coolly escaped. The two killers who were in overcoats walked out first, with their hands raised. The two who were dressed as policemen, with their guns pointed at the "criminals", escorted their charges to the parked police car. To witnesses who had dared to look toward the sound of the gunshots, it appeared that the crime was already solved and the police had already made an arrest.[25]

The crime was not solved, of course, and it never was. Also unsolved were the 800 or so other murders that took place in Chicago during the prohibition years of 1920 to 1933. Most of the killings in New York, Detroit, Buffalo and a host of other cities went unsolved as well. Nationally, homicides rose, during prohibition, from seven per 100,000 to almost ten per 100,000. These killings had to stop if the Mafia was to survive. Lucky Luciano's Commission was the ticket to controlling a lot of those problems. And once the guys got organized, they stayed organized, as they are to this day.[26]

CORRUPTION

Lucky Luciano was as smart as he was smartly dressed. He knew that selling booze and organizing mobsters was a good start, but that he needed the cooperation of the authorities in order to stay in business. There was simply no way to hide the thousands of speakeasies from the local beat cops. Similarly, someone had to look the other way when trucks, trains, boats and cars brought Irish Whisky to Italian saloons.

Fiorella H. LaGuardia, a New York congressman, spoke of this corruption to the US Senate in 1926. He told that august chamber that he had been told of middle class prohibition agents who had chauffeurs for their cars! He also estimated that in excess of a million dollars a year was transferred from gangsters to cooperative agents at all levels: from the Feds down to the local yokels.[27]

Whether congressman LaGuardia's numbers are accurate or not is irrelevant. The fact is, the process of prohibition was ripe with opportunity and rife with corruption. From the beat cop and the Federal agents to the judges and the country's politicians, working stiffs and wealthy alike were more than willing to look the other way when it came to liquor. They took the candy and they drank the brandy.

On the front lines of this hypocritical bureaucracy, where the booze was transported, distributed and ultimately consumed, were the police, Bureau of Prohibition agents, US Customs servicemen and Border Patrolmen. These guys were underpaid and the lure of big money was hard to resist. That lure resulted in the dismissal of more than a tenth of the agents from the Prohibition Bureau. And that was undoubtedly the tip of the iceberg. Certainly, the authorities did not catch all of the offenders. Most likely, they did not catch even the majority of those who looked the other way for a fee.[28]

Part of the problem was the meager salary that the agents received. The average national income in 1922 was $3,143 and in 1923 it skyrocketed to $3,227. The salary of Prohibition agents ranged from $1,200 to $2,500 for 98 per cent of the Bureau. By 1930, the entry level salary was a whopping $2,300, two-thirds of the national average. For the Coast Guard, it was even less. In the Guard, enlisted men were paid the princely sum of $36 (each and every month!). However, they did receive three squares and a roof over their head, courtesy of Uncle Sam. Free uniforms were thrown in for good measure. Nonetheless, with next to nothing in their wallets, many agents took bribes from the bootleggers. The low salaries do not excuse the corruption but human nature being what it is, the likelihood of rich gangsters being able to pay off underpaid agents should have been fairly obvious.[29]

And it was not just the blue collar Federal guys with their hand in the till. The whole system joined in. Cops, courts and corrupt politicians augmented their salaries with Mafia money. Bribes were common and it wasn't just the common men who accepted them. Henry Anderson, the top dog in the Prohibition bureau, said that agents being paid to look the other way was pervasive in his department. But bribes were just one strategy in this new business model. The mob added a couple of more interesting twists where elected officials were concerned.[30]

Twist number one was ironically democratic. An elected official was simply beaten at the polls. The mob backed their guy with a bulging campaign chest. They released scandalous stories about the incumbent and they made very sure that their guy got a lot of votes. In this twist, the mob got rid of a pain in the neck prosecutor or justice-crazed judge and replaced him with a gangster goon who would do as he was told. Twist number two was somewhat easier. In this strategy, the bad guys killed the good guys. Less sophisticated, yes, but no less effective.[31]

THE PRODUCT

As we saw with smuggling and corruption in government entities, it is fair to say that the bootleggers were not law abiding citizens. The quality of the liquor that they sold was affected by this disregard for the law. The quality was affected in two ways. First, ordinary citizens were enlisted to illegally make "bathtub gin" in their homes. Second, along with killing the occasional competitor and bribing the local authorities, the smugglers ignored lawful consumer protections designed to safeguard the American public. The bootleggers routinely "cut" legitimate alcohol with ineffective and often dangerous substitute liquids.[32]

Issue one was home brewing. Throughout the Prohibition era, people all over the country turned into home-based alcohol manufacturers. Ordinary citizens became brewmeisters and vintners. Some of that production was for personal consumption but more often it was for profit. In many cases, the booze was brewed at the behest of the bootleggers. If, on the other hand, one was inclined to sell the liquor himself, he had to be mindful not to step on the spit polished shoes of the local gangsters.[33]

Unless, of course, the gangsters themselves were involved. Often the equipment for brewing the booze was supplied by the gangsters themselves; sometimes for free, sometimes for a small, one-time, pay it and shut up, fee for the liquor kit. The home brew was made for the mobsters for resale at the speakeasies. Everyone was a winner. Except, from time to time, the consumer. There was no inspection, no quality control in the bathtub where the gin was ginned, to safeguard the speakeasy swingers.[34]

Quality control was at the heart of the second dangerous component of alcohol supply as well. The inconsistent potency of mob supplied alcoholic beverages was a real problem. With no inspection by government agencies, bootleggers sought to increase profits by selling booze that was cut with other liquids. This unregulated adulteration of alcohol led to a product that was often dangerous. The homemade alcohol was as much as 50 per cent stronger than the pre-Prohibition product. That was a very dangerous situation for the unsuspecting consumer.[35]

Today, the safeguards provided by government agencies see to it that customers of legitimate alcohol manufacturers can expect to get a safe, consistent product from the shelf of their local liquor store. Customers of prohibition mobsters had no such guarantee. The booze that made its way to the lips of speakeasy denizens was as good or as bad as the seller could get away with.

This cutting of the end product was very dangerous. Some of the liquor was cut with wood alcohol. This seriously dangerous liquid was indiscernible from "good" alcohol both in taste and effect. As wood alcohol was less expensive than whisky, adding it to the whisky reduced the cost per gallon to the retailers. This contamination led to thousands of deaths of Prohibition partiers. Some potentially dead people were "saved" by the fact that they went blind before they drank enough to die. If neither of those calamities got one in its clutches, drinking wood alcohol could potentially damage one's internal organs, including, among others, the brain and the kidneys. You need those. [36]

But people drank it anyway. And the suppliers were more than happy to supply those drinks, especially when those drinks were the hard stuff. The hard stuff was less risky to smuggle into the country because it didn't take up as much room as beer did. Beer came in barrels and had to be transported in trucks. Whisky came in bottles and could be transported in cars, boats or boots. [37]

Also, the importers got more bang for the buck with spirits. That is, a pint of whisky fetched a much prettier penny than did a pint of suds. And it got even better. To hide the often near-nasty to pure-nasty taste of the cut booze they were serving, the bar owners cut it further, this time with sweeteners. They invented the cocktail! Talk about killing two birds while getting both stoned! This was genius. Using soda water, ginger ale, etc., disguised the awful taste and cut the booze a second time, increasing profits further. What a country![38]

THE COST

Notwithstanding the serious nature of the preceding discussions, the *cost* of Prohibition was perhaps the most significant part of the problem. America got hit coming and going. On one hand, the Treasury lost a mountain of incoming dollars. The manufacturers did not pay income tax on their sales to wholesalers. The wholesalers did not pay income tax on their sales to retailers. The retailers did not pay income tax or sales tax on the sweetened, distorted booze that they poured for the easy speakers in the speakeasies.

On the other hand, prevention also came at a cost. An entire new agency had to be created and funded. Police departments, the Coast Guard, and Customs had to expand their employee rosters. To handle the flood of prosecutions and incarcerations, the government needed more attorneys, judges, courtrooms, jails and prisons. Sound expensive? It was.

Lastly, many Americans lost the jobs that they had held in the liquor industry. The Treasury potentially lost the income tax from this set of workers as well. As they were working under the table, there was no official record of their earnings for tax reporting purposes.

Significant intakes of Excise taxes on alcohol dried up as a result of Prohibition. In 1926, Fiorella LaGuardia seemed to agree, testifying to Congress that the loss was over a billion dollars annually. That was an exaggeration, of course, politicians being what they are, but he did have a point. The fact was, in 1919, the government collected more than $450 billion from taxing the sale of alcohol. This could easily have been $500 million by 1926, making LaGuardia at least half right. [39]

The other side of the silver coin was the cost of prohibiting the use of demon rum in the several States of the United States. The cost went up as the years went by. As the chart below illustrates, the initial cost was three million dollars. A decade later, that cost had more than tripled. The exact expenditures, as reported, included the cost of policing drugs. Those excess costs were approximately ten percent of the totals reported. Those totals (rounded) were:

YEAR	EXPENDITURES
1920	$ 2,966,000
1921	7,035,000
1922	7,327,000
1923	8,994,000
1924	8,457,000
1925	10,499,000
1926	10,995,000
1927	12,465,000

1928	12,939,000
1929	13,645,000
1930	14,949,900[40]

Other services spent their share of America's hard earned dollars as well. The Customs Service added some 50 per cent to their employment rolls. The cost of the department went up more than 100 per cent. The Coast Guard had even greater growth: nearly 200 per cent increase in personnel and a 500 per cent increase in costs.[41]

But, of course, it did not stop there. Once the agents caught their man, the judges, juries and jailers had to have their say. By 1930, the number of court cases for violations of the Prohibition Act had increased eightfold from the beginning of Prohibition. The courtrooms of America were clogged. In 1923, *Time* reported that over 40 per cent of the Federal government's prosecutions were related to Prohibition. Five years later, there were 75,000 cases in 52 weeks of the year. Fast forward four more years and the busts were up to 80,000 per annum. Convictions went up 1000 percent in the second half decade of Prohibition. The courts were drowning in a sea of liquor litigation.[42]

And, not surprisingly, the prisons soon found themselves floundering as well. The sheer volume of prisoners overwhelmed them. Between the years of 1914 and 1932, the number of Federal prisoners increased from 3,000 to almost 27,000. Atlanta Penitentiary and Leavenworth were populated at more than double capacity. Sing Sing had to farm out some of its inmates to another facility.[43]

This came at a cost, of course. Prior to getting his stock market crash/depression era walking papers, President Hoover attempted to alleviate the housing problem by building six new prisons.

Those facilities and their cousins required a mountain of cash for guards, food, clothing and health care for the inmates. As a result, the Federal government's prison budget rose a staggering 1,000 percent during the years surrounding Prohibition.[44]

While some jobs were created at those prisons, as well as with the enforcement agencies, many other jobs were lost by those who had made their living in the liquor industry. Let's start with the little guys. Everyone in the factory lost their jobs - The bottlers, the shipping clerks, the maintenance crews, the secretaries – everyone. All the support people got a ticket to the unemployment ball as well. That included hardworking, honest American truck drivers, salesmen, liquor store clerks, bartenders and cocktail waitresses. Of course, some of these people remained in the liquor business but they instantly became criminals. They kept their old jobs at the risk of incarceration where, ironically, they could have been watched over by one of the guys who took one of the aforementioned new jobs with the penal institutions.[45]

And what about the big boys? Owners of the breweries were faced with the same dilemma as the grunts on the shop floor. Should they close up shop and look for a job or go underground, as criminals, and continue making booze? Liquor store owners likewise had to close up shop after selling off whatever they had left on the shelves. Saloon doors stopped swinging as the owners walked out for the last time. Wine makers and brew masters also

found no legitimate market for their hard earned talents.
46

And, of course, this would cost the government plenty. As all of these folks had become unemployed, they no longer would pay any income tax. The former owners, who were instantly put out of business, would no longer calculate sales taxes as a percent of their revenue and tender those monies to the Federal and State governments. Some of these men, bosses and workers alike, who had been honorably and gainfully employed before the passing of the 18th Amendment, would need to look to those same governments for assistance in meeting their financial and familial obligations.

UNINTENDED CONSEQUENCES

Some of the former liquor industry workers, rather than go on the dole, would continue to work in the new liquor industry. They would, therefore, become criminals, often working for large criminal organizations. In that, they joined in the endeavors of other, more proactive, members of the underbelly of American life. At the beginning of Prohibition, thefts and burglaries increased by 9 percent. Homicides combined with assault and battery for an increase of 13 percent. Homicides, when measured alone, went up from about 6.8 per 100,000 in 1920 to 10 per 100,000 in 1933. About 100 of those homicides were Prohibition Bureau agents.[47]

It is noteworthy that Prohibition did very little to reduce drinking. There was a dramatic initial drop in consumption followed by a zig-zag upward trend which reached 80 percent of pre-Prohibition rates by 1929. Despite a huge negative change in government revenue intake and expenditures as well as to the American quality of life, drinking continued virtually unabated.

Lastly, drinking liquor in speakeasies had the "Glamour Factor." Young people went to these clubs because they were cool. And it wasn't just the guys. "Respectable" women, who were not generally found in pre-Prohibition saloons, streamed into the Prohibition watering holes. The mob, which was not generally in touch with their feminist side, were most definitely in touch with its capitalist side. They decided that girl dollars counted just as much as boy dollars. And, to make things better, boys spent their boy dollars on the girls! The dramatic upswing of female drinking was yet another unintended consequence of the "Noble Experiment."[48]

Prohibition of alcohol was a colossal failure. It cost the government a lot of money, both in lost revenue and in wasted expenditures. That money was collected instead, in piles and piles of cash, by gangsters. To get and keep that cash, those gangsters killed one another, often in spectacular fashion. American citizens became instant criminals by working in the liquor industry. Elected officials and law enforcement agents were corrupted. We will see a remarkable parallel to these conditions in the discussion of the war on drugs that follows.

DRUGS

Just as with alcohol, all of the recreational drugs in popular use today, such as marijuana, opium (from which heroin is made) and cocaine, were once legal. In most cases, they were criminalized by laws passed in the early 20th century by folks who were genuinely trying to create a better society. Unfortunately, as with the prohibition of alcohol, the criminalization of drugs brought with it some very unfortunate side effects.

One of those insidious side effects was the creation of a huge black market for the drugs. The demand in that market has been met by many providers, including: powerful international cartels, international terrorists and street gangs in cities all across America.

Meeting that demand has meant a lot of money for the suppliers. But as Economics 101 taught us, that big money also created a crisis of competition among suppliers. In order to keep control of a particular fiefdom, each neo-feudal, drug smuggling, dope peddling organization had to demonstrate efficiency in two skill sets – Murder and Corruption.

Once those two protective devices were in place, the suppliers could concentrate on the supply itself. In order to increase their profits, the suppliers routinely "cut" their product with foreign substances. The predictable unpredictability in the potency of the product could be, and often was, a very dangerous game for the consumer.

The whole process has also been an extremely costly game for all Americans, drug consumers and "straights" alike. The income taxes and sales taxes that are generated by the sale of legal products are not generated in the case of the sale of drugs. Instead, those dollars line the pockets of criminals and terrorists. And compounding the cost to honest, hard working American citizens is the cost of the arrest, conviction and incarceration of drug offenders. That cost has skyrocketed since America declared war on drugs. Prisons have filled to overflowing. Some States have begun to farm out that overflow to other states. In other cases, authorities have considered early releases for prisoners who were convicted of non-violent crimes. Crimes like possession and use of drugs! Go figure.

Of course, all of those problems would go by the wayside simply by legalizing drugs. Without the cash to pay their minions, the criminal drug organizations would be reduced to a fraction of their current size and power.

THE HISTORY OF DRUGS IN THE U.S.

There are many ways to get high in America. In the preceding chapter, we discussed the only one that is currently designed to provide a legal high in the United States, alcohol. The rest of the lot will provide the high but are not legal to possess, let alone use, in the United States. Examples of those intoxicating substances would include marijuana, opium, cocaine, ecstasy, LSD, barbiturates and amphetamines (although there are legal uses for these last two). It could also include legitimate products which enterprising drug users have found to be intoxicating, such as cough syrup and glue. To discuss all those and their unnamed hundreds of hybrids would take volumes. We will focus on the first three, marijuana, opium and cocaine.

MARIJUANA

Marijuana has had various uses around the globe for thousands of years. It appeared in a medical book in China as early as 2,737 BC. Throughout the ensuing centuries, marijuana was used for various legal purposes in various locations on the map. Some of those places were China, India, Europe and, more to our point, the United States of America.[49]

Marijuana has had many legal uses over this time. One of the most common uses was to make rope and clothing from the hemp (marijuana) plant. This usage of the "evil weed" goes back to the Chinese as well. However, this Asian native plant was transplanted all over the world, eventually making its way to North America. There, in 1619, the Jamestown Colony, in Virginia passed the first law in North America that related to marijuana. Ironically, this law required that farmers in the colony *grow* hemp. Not only was it legal, it was in the best interests of the colony to have ample supplies of the plant from which the colonists made clothing and rope. This government support would repeat itself during World War II. As part of the war effort, the United States government planted hemp to make into cordage. These fields were made necessary by the Japanese, who controlled the Asian hemp fields during that conflict. [50]

Peacetime uses of marijuana abounded as well. For example, in business, it had long been used (and still is) as a component of birdseed. It was also used in paint products and lamp oil. As a treat, in the 19th century, it was used as an ingredient in maple sugar hashish candy, sold in the United States by the Gunjah Wallah Company.[51]

It has been, of course, also used as an intoxicant for a few thousand years. In America, in the post Civil War period, we saw the rise of Turkish smoking parlors, including a popular puffing parlor at America's Centennial Exposition in Philadelphia. The 20th century saw a gradual increase in marijuana use. The early part of the century saw the smoking of weed by workers who came up from Mexico. There was also a good deal of pot being smoked by Afro-Americans in New Orleans (this was a partial explanation for the popularity of that evil, satanic music – jazz!). Later, we will see, based on these examples of "the evil weed" among minorities, that racism was used to help outlaw marijuana use in the United States.[52]

But as the new century unfolded, more and more "good" (white) folks started puffing the pipe, including one president who was apparently too dumb to inhale. It was outlawed in 1937. Nonetheless, by the 1950s, Americans, some of them called beatniks, were still smoking pot. They were followed a decade later by the hippies of the sixties. Everyone from heroes to homeless was lighting up the magical weed. Marijuana had gone mainstream.

But it had really been mainstream for a very long time. Marijuana was used to treat a myriad of medical complaints, for centuries. In China, it was used as medicine to combat the effects of various diseases, including gout and malaria. It was also used for pain relief. In 1894, the India Hemp Commission learned that the drug was also helpful in the treatment of pain, hay fever, diarrhea and dysentery. The Commission listed some twenty-one different medical conditions that were reported to be alleviated by the consumption of cannabis.[53]

And it was similarly used in the United States. In Ohio, in 1860, the State Medical Society formed a committee to study marijuana. This committee also noted that marijuana (they called it cannabis) was medically useful for pain, palsy, epilepsy and others. In 1857, Dr. John Bell used the substance to treat mental disorders. Marijuana was an oft used pain reliever until it was displaced in 1901 by the wonder drug, aspirin. Decades later, in the late twentieth century we saw a rise in the decriminalization of pot in order that it could be used to relieve the symptoms of glaucoma and nausea, the latter often a side effect of cancer fighting chemotherapy. Some Americans are unhappy with these "excuses" for pot use but I doubt if any of the doubters are actually suffering from either of those conditions.[54]

So why was it criminalized? Folks got scared. The government told them a couple of tall tales. The first "reason" was racist. This was an easy sell in early 20th century America. It was blamed on the damned Mexicans that were eating up west coast jobs (this sounds like today but it was a hundred years ago!). The second "reason" was to save the young people of America. As we will see later, this gateway drug hypothesis helped make weed illegal.[55]

So, irrespective of the occasional lax law on marijuana, the 20th century saw a systematic criminalization of the weed. However, the drug was still in high demand for those who still demanded a high. Ergo, as with alcohol prohibition, this led to a very profitable black market. The folks who were (and are) involved with that supply were not (and are not) nice people. They included various international drug cartels, terrorists and, of course, your local gangs.

OPIUM

These same gangsters would eventually profit hugely from the sale of opium as well but that trade would take centuries to develop. Opium, like marijuana, has a long history. It began as a recreational and medicinal drug in the Middle East and moved to Asia and eventually found its way to Europe and the United States.[56]

Like marijuana, opium comes from a plant, in this case the poppy. The poppy plant was grown as early as 3400 BC in Mesopotamia. Opium spread throughout the Middle East and eventually to Asia. There it found a home in India.[57]

And India figured prominently in the spread of opium use. The Asian subcontinent had been colonized by the British. Great Britain, and indeed the rest of Europe (and America as well), had developed a large demand for opium. In many cases, the demand was for recreational use. World famous authors John Keats and Elizabeth Barrett Browning, for example, along with other literati luminaries, ingested opiates for a chemical "night on the town." Opium put the "in" in "intoxicant" in 19th century Europe![58]

In addition to recreational uses, however, medical uses for the drug were also discovered at that time. In 1680, Thomas Sydenham created Laudanum from a combination of opiates and sherry. Laudanum was a popular liquid for relieving various complaints, sort of a 17th century traveling salesman's elixir – good for what ails you. The next advancement in the medicinal use of opiates came out of Germany. In that country, in 1803, Friedrich Sertuerner developed morphine from opium. That drug continues to be used today as a very potent pain killer. In 1874, C.R Wright, an Englishman, converted morphine to heroin.[59]

Englishmen, along with their continental cohorts, wanted their opium. In 1830, 22,000 pounds of opium was imported to Great Britain. And India, a British colony, was the perfect place to grow the popular poppy and a perfect place from which to ship it.[60]

The British East India Company, which had been given a monopoly on opium growth by the British Governor, made a lot of money by doing just that. And it got even better for the EIC. They began exporting opium to China, despite the prohibition of the drug in that country. [61]

That Chinese trade was one-third of what became known as the "Triangular Trade." The triangular trade was a three way exchange of money and products that was promoted by the English government. As one leg of the triangle, the EIC, with the blessing of the English government, sent illegal opium to the Chinese. The second leg was the shipment of Chinese tea to England. The last leg of the triangle was the shipment of English goods to India, thus completing the triangle of trade.[62]

The EIC portion of the triangular trade was very profitable but also somewhat short lived. Their exclusive control of the illicit drug was cancelled in 1834. At that point, the East India Company had a number of competitors for its monstrous profits. In addition to the predictable British competitors, Americans were waiting in line to make a profit selling drugs to the Chinese.[63]

But it was the British alone who would ensure that the trade continued. They fought two "Opium Wars", creatively called the First Opium War and the Second Opium War, to keep the triangular trade triangulating.

These two wars were a direct result of the Chinese government's attempts to *eliminate* the opium trade in their country. The Chinese government was trying to eradicate opium from their country but the English were having nothing of it. The Chinese government sent a representative, Lin Ze-xu, to Canton, the main entry point for foreign opium into China. Lin seized millions in opium and had it burned. He also banned foreign traders from importing or exporting in Canton. The English were not happy. [64]

The British struck back in the First Opium War. Starting in 1839, they began sinking Chinese ships. The Chinese junks and primitive weapons, arrows (seriously!) and muskets, were simply no match for the modern might of the British armed forces. By 1842, the British had won significant naval and land victories. The Chinese were required to ransom back their own city of Canton and cede the city of Hong Kong to the British. The Chinese would not get that city back for over one hundred and fifty years. The Chinese were also forced to sign the "unequal" treaties which gave the western countries control of much of the Chinese coast. [65]

Despite a huge post-war increase in the sale of opium to China, the west wasn't through arranging sales territories in China. The original treaty that ended the First War was renegotiated after 12 years. The Chinese stalled for a couple of years but the British finally pushed the issue in 1856. The Chinese had boarded a foreign ship, the *Arrow*, looking for smuggling. In a calculated over-response to that action, the British, along with the Americans and the French, attacked the Chinese. Again, the superior forces of the western powers won the day. The Chinese were forced to open more ports to the western traders. The Chinese subsequently legalized opium.[66]

The western powers had succeeded in forcing opium sales and its accompanying addictive consumption on an unwilling but ultimately powerless China. To support the demand in China, as well as the huge consumption in Europe and the United States, western powers oversaw the cultivation of the poppy in India and Bengal. Competitors to those growers popped up in China and Turkey. Opium production and use became one of the first global enterprises.[67]

Everybody continued making money into the 20th century, but then, the mood of the country began to change. As the new century dawned, heroin use had risen to the point that the country began to take notice. And they did not like what they saw. In addition, just as we saw with marijuana, racism raised its ugly head. Opium smoking Chinese immigrants were coming into the western United States in hordes and supplying cheap labor, primarily for the railroads. Of course, those were jobs that white folks wanted. The Chinese had to go and the Chinese opium had to go with them.[68]

As a result, opium was outlawed in the United States. The first anti-drug legislation, the Pure Food and Drug Act, was passed in 1903. Within twenty years, the drug went underground. With the legal outlets closed up and the demand still wide open, smugglers got into the game in the Chinatown section of New York City. In time, that black market was absorbed by the Mafia and eventually street gangs in every city in the nation[69]

However, those domestic organizations were restricted to procurement and sales alone. Supply of the poppy's magic, in the 20th century, continued to be an international affair. That process also became controlled by large, powerful organizations as the century progressed. The Taliban, in Afghanistan, used drug money to help fund their government. In the late seventies, "Mexican Mud (heroin)" began mainlining into America. By the 1990's, Columbian drug lords began to send heroin to the United States as well. Later in the decade, the drug distributors of Southeast Asia became major players.[70]

COCAINE

Cocaine, as you have probably guessed by now, has been used for centuries. In South America, the plant (yes, of course, it comes from a plant), had both religious and medical uses. The ancient South Americans chewed the leaf of the coca plant for their health and also for religious reasons. They believed that their gods had created the drug for that use. When the Europeans discovered the coca plant, they used it both for recreational and medicinal purposes. The Americans got in line right behind the Europeans.[71]

High in the Andes Mountains of South America, the ancient denizens of those upper altitudes cultivated the coca plant for hundreds of years. The effects of chewing the leaves of the plant helped the South American mountain dwellers live and work in the thin air. Those people found that chewing the coca plant was beneficial in several ways. It helped them ease their hunger and, of course, gave them lots of energy. And, as we said, it was recognized as a "special" kind of herb and was used in the local religions.[72]

The Spaniards came into contact with the coca plant when they began their conquest of South America. Their first impression of the plant was that it was Satan's work and they prohibited its use. However, the Spaniards soon realized that they got more production from the local workers when those workers chewed the coca leaf. The effects of the drug allowed the local laborers to keep in the silver mines well beyond the eight hours a day we are often unable to handle here in the 21st century. So, capitalism (actually mercantilism, but we're really splitting hairs here) being what it is, the Spaniards let the laborers harvest their coca as long as the Spaniards continued to reap the benefits.[73]

The Spaniard's next step was to export the drug to Europe. Surely the civilized world could make use of the magical plant of the Andes. There was a problem, however. The plant did not travel well. By the time it got to Europe, the numbing effect of the coca leaf had waned. It was not until the middle of the nineteenth century that chemists were able to isolate the narcotic from the plant.[74]

That isolation allowed physicians to use the drug on their patients. One of its early uses was in eye surgery. Prior to the use of cocaine, some patients had to submit to surgery without moving an inch! That was obviously not an ideal surgical technique. Cocaine was also used in cough medicines and toothache relievers. As late as 1914, the drug, in its various tonic forms, could be purchased over the counter at your neighborhood drug store.[75]

But Cocaine's real appeal was recreational. It was sold in cigarettes and wine. A particular French wine contained 7.2 mg per ounce. Cocaine found its way into other products as well, most notably, Coca-Cola. There was generally a 60 mg dose of cocaine in each bottle of ice cold refreshment. Today's coke has no coke in it at all.[76]

But Europeans in the 19th century did have coke in themselves. It became a very popular drug. Unlike today, it wasn't snorted back then. They usually drank it, like alcohol. Call it a coketail. However, the powder form did eventually win out. The magic dust soon found its way across the pond to America, where it was equally popular.[77]

Helping to popularize the drug was the use of it by one Sigmund Freud. The father of psychoanalysis experimented with the drug to determine if it would be useful in treating his patients. Uh-huh. Sure, Sigmund. Anyway, Freud discovered that cocaine could be used to combat depression. Yeah, we could have guessed that. However, he also noted positive effects in its use with problematic stomachs and coughing. Only to a point, though. Freud also had to agree that cocaine's beneficial properties were inconsistent and that it was, therefore, contraindicated for general prescription to the public.[78]

But widespread use came to be, nonetheless. Despite 20th century laws prohibiting its use, Cocaine eventually became a very popular drug indeed. Until the 1970s, however, the drug was not a major player in the United States. The drug's popularity began to soar in the late seventies and into the early eighties. The problem with Cocaine, if you put aside the significant detrimental effect on the user's health, appearance, job, friends, etc., was the cost. The stuff was expensive.

But crack cocaine was not expensive. Some "genius" figured out how to convert the powder into a more powerful and more addicting form of Cocaine called crack.

Cocaine dealers could stretch the drug a lot farther when it was converted to crack than when it was sold as powder. And that was important. The price for the poor man's coke went down. Cocaine had become everybody's high. While the elite could still buy their cocaine in powder and do lines at exclusive parties, the poor could afford their coke in chunks, to be savored in a pipe, behind the liquor store, in a cardboard box.[79]

The price went down, for crack addicts at least, but the demand did not. In order to supply that demand, bad guys got involved. One of the most prominent organizations to import Cocaine into the United States was the Medellin cartel. We will look at this cartel and some of its competitors in a later chapter but suffice it to say that a lot of money was made and a lot of murders were committed.[80]

Before moving on, I'd like to note that the early laws that banned coke were, in part, racially motivated. I know you're shocked but it's true! The New York Times claimed that coke-head Afro-Americans were responsible for the lion's share of attacks on white women. In the South, a few police departments stopped using .32 caliber bullets, opting for .38 instead. They believed that cocaine made Afro-Americans invulnerable to the 32s. Stupid, of course, but this does lead us to a discussion of the other anti-drug laws that were passed by the Federal Government in the 20th century. Note that the individual States passed their own laws as well but we will not delve that deep into the morass.[81]

THE LAWS

At the beginning of the 20th century, in response to the trumped up racial fears and the perceived tendency of America's youth to rapidly become drug addicts, the United States began enacting laws to prohibit the use of recreational drugs. Several of those laws are listed in the table below.

Selected Federal Anti-Drug Laws in the United States

YEAR	TITLE	PURPOSE
1906	Pure Food and Drug Act	Set penalties for adulterated drugs
1914	Harrison Narcotics Act	Imposed a tax for drug suppliers. Set penalties for violation
1922	Narcotic Drug and Export Act	Banned non-medicinal use of narcotics
1924	Heroin Act	Banned Heroin manufacture
1937	Marijuana Tax Act	Imposed a tax for Marijuana suppliers. Set penalties.
1942	Opium Poppy Control Act	Banned Poppy farming without a license
1951	Boggs Amendment to the Harrison Narcotic Act	Set mandatory penalties for narcotic use.
1956	Narcotics Control Act	Set more sever penalties
1965	Drug Abuse Control Amendments	Controls on various drugs, including LSD for the first time.
1970	Comprehensive Drug Abuse and Control Act	Updated previous laws.
1986	Analogue (Designer Drug) Act	Banned drugs with similar structures to existing illicit drugs

82

This table is not a complete list of all the Federal legislation related to recreational drug use. It also does not include any legislation passed by the individual states. It does, however, provide somewhat of a guideline to narcotic control in the United States, from the early attempts at taxation to the later bills that banned the use of the drugs entirely. We will investigate a few of those laws in detail next.

The first national anti-drug act of the 20th century was the Pure Food and Drug Act, enacted in 1906. It prevented "the manufacture, sale or transportation of adulterated …. foods, drugs, medicines and liquors." The Act was written to control the quality of food and medicines within the United States as well as any food and medicines exported from the States. This Act was a consumer protection bill that required all food and medicines to contain only what that were supposed to contain. Watering down products or adding potentially harmful filler to products in order to maximize profits were the targets of the Act.[83]

Violations of this Act were deemed as a misdemeanor. The manufacture or sale of adulterated goods were punishable by a maximum fine of $500 for the first offense ($1000 for subsequent offenses) or one year in jail or both. Importation of such goods into the country carried penalties of $200 for the first offense and $300 for subsequent offenses or one year in jail or both. The law did not, however, ban or even restrict the use of recreational drugs.[84]

The Harrison Act (1914) did not ban recreational use of drugs either. But it did begin the slide down the slippery slope. Rather than an outright ban on drugs, the Harrison Act created a "special tax all persons who produce, import, manufacture … sell, or give away opium or coca leaves." The Act also provided penalties for non-compliance.[85]

To be compliant, a person who intended to sell drugs had to "register with the collector of internal Revenue" and pay the special tax of $1 per year. Yes, I said $1. The United States of America was not going to get rich enforcing this Act! The Act also required that prescriptions be used for the possession or distribution of narcotics. The intent was to regulate drugs while not technically regulating them. As drug dealers and addicts were unlikely to provide their names and addresses to the authorities on a license application, any further sale or use of narcotics by those citizens became crimes against the State.[86]

And, of course, those crimes had penalties. Any violation of the Harrison Act carried with it a maximum fine of $200 or a maximum jail sentence of 5 years in jail or both. In order to enforce those penalties, the Act authorized "agents, deputy collectors, inspectors, chemists, assistant chemists, clerks and messengers." In order to carry out these requirements, $150,000 was provided under the act.[87]

The enforcement of the Act had unfortunate, though predictable, effects on the American people. In late 1915, an article in *American Medicine* revealed that users, with no legal avenue to get their fix, had to buy the dope on the black market. Both the user and the supplier became criminals overnight. In 1918, the Secretary of the Treasury appointed a committee to look into the effects of the Harrison Act. The committee found that "The 'dope peddlers' appeared to have established a national organization, smuggling drugs in through seaports or cross the Canadian or Mexican borders." The parallels with alcohol prohibition cannot be ignored, both in the generation of an illegal organization and the ports of entry of the illicit products.[88]

A similar Act, this time targeting Marijuana, was passed in 1937. It was called, of course, The Marihuana Act of 1937. As with the Harrison Act, this ban on the drug was not technically a ban at all. It simply imposed a tax of $24 a year on "importers, manufacturers and compounders of marihuana." Growers only had to pay $1. Any supplier who was not in a medical field had to put up $3. But the real tax was on the product, $1 per ounce. That was a lot in 1937. Unregistered persons had to pay $100 an ounce. That was a small fortune in 1937.[89]

In addition, as with the Harrison Act, in order to legally grow, sell, import, etc, marihuana, the grower, seller, etc, had to register with the Feds. Again, not a popular game plan for addicts and their suppliers. Nonetheless, failure to supply or consume weed without registering was illegal and came with those now commonplace penalties. This time it was a $2,000 fine, five years in jail, or both.[90]

The size of those penalties were, in part, due to "facts" that were given in a statement by H.J Anslinger, Commissioner of Narcotics, during Congressional hearings on April 27, 1937. Anslinger told the congressmen that "those who are habitually accustomed to use [pot]... develop a delirious rage after its administration." He goes on to say "Its use frequently leads to insanity." It gets better. He also informed the illustrious denizens of Capitol Hill that "Social dangers that ensue from the use of marihuana are comparable to those that result from heroin." He went on to claim "that the majority of users are ignorant and inexperienced youngsters and members of the lowest strata of humanity." With that kind of "expert" testimony, the Act was sure to pass. [91]

Yet another "expert" opinion helped fuel the further expansion of narcotics laws. This opinion came from our friend Mr. Anslinger and a second witness, one Representative Boggs. In Congressional hearings prior to enactment of the Boggs Act of 1951, these two men came up with a new reason for outlawing drugs – the effect. Commissioner Anslinger testified that "over 50 percent of these young addicts started on marihuana smoking. They started there and graduated to heroin." Representative Boggs had his back. He told the members of the House that "Our younger people usually start on the road ... to drug addiction by smoking marihuana. They then graduate into narcotic drugs – cocaine, morphine and heroin."[92]

This gateway thing had its obvious flaws. For instance, a paper by Dr. Harris Isbell was filed with the House. It said, in part, that pot smokers would not hurt anyone. The paper went on to say that there was no evidence that pot smoking was a path to crime. Dr. Isbell also said that it was his opinion that stopping the use of pot would not be difficult. He said that he believed that quitting pot would be easier than quitting cigarette smoking. Despite this expert testimony that pot was not addicting and relatively harmless, the gateway effect became a "fact" that is still in use today.[93]

The gateway claim led to the next assaults on the drug culture, The Boggs Act and the Narcotics Control Act. The Boggs Act, which was serious business indeed, was enacted in 1951 (the year that I was born, although I'm convinced that the two events are simply a coincidence). This Act mixed marijuana and narcotics together for the first time. It also placed into law mandatory sentencing for a second offense. Judges were no longer free to give probation to drug users. In 1956, The Narcotics Control Act raised the bar considerably. First offenders (for possession only) could expect a 2 year stretch in the pen. A third offender would get ten years and up to a $20,000 fine! Suppliers were now looking at 5 years for a first offense and 10 years for a second bust. In 1965, the passing of The Drug Abuse Control Amendments went a step further. These increased the control over "amphetamines, barbiturates and LSD." This was the first time LSD had been criminalized.[94]

But not all Federal Legislation was punitive. In 1972, the Drug Abuse Office and Treatment Act provided funds for "prevention and treatment." The Alcohol and Drug Abuse Education Amendments of 1978 and The 1980 Drug Abuse Prevention, Treatment, and Rehabilitation Amendments both dealt with Federal funding for education and treatment. In 1984, The Drug Offenders Act furthered that effort. With the feds pushing for treatment over incarceration, it is no surprise that the 80's were the beginning of the rehab phenomena.[95]

In keeping with this softer approach to the war on drug users, the Obama administration, in 2009, issued a policy statement that put a stop to federal raids on medical marijuana providers. That policy put a stop to the paradox that had been created when thirteen states reduced or eliminated the penalties on marijuana used for medical purposes. Those new state laws were in direct conflict with Federal law.[96]

Leading the list of states with new laws, predictably, was California. And leading the Californians - Los

Angeles. Marijuana houses in LA popped up on every corner. In addition to patients who really needed the drug, aging hippies and youthful experimenters, with no medical conditions save a craving to get mellow, had a possible quasi-legal avenue to buy pot and get high. The revolution had begun!

SMUGGLING

As soon as the Federal Government, and the State Governments for that matter, passed legislation outlawing the possession and sale of drugs, the bad guys' eyes lit up. These guys knew a gold mine when they saw one. Laws were for suckers. Profits were waiting, and criminals from Burma to the Bronx were lined up to get their piece of the pie. Everyone along the food chain took a chunk of the change except, of course, the Treasuries of any country where the drugs were sold (actually, a couple did, but we'll look at that later!).

The drugs came in, and still come in, from the same places that booze came in from during Prohibition – Canada, Mexico and the Caribbean. The bulk of the booty comes in from Mexico but drug suppliers from all over the world have found other pipelines and very unique methods of entry into the United States.[97]

A significant portion of the drugs imported into the United States comes from Mexico. In 2000, the DEA reported that "half of the cocaine ... the majority of marijuana and a significant portion of heroin consumed in the United States emanates from Mexico ... Mexican drug organizations ... produce 85 percent of the methamphetamine available in the U.S." Not all of those drugs originated in Mexico. By the early 1990s, the South American drug cartels of the 1980s had subcontracted the importation of their product into the United States to Mexican drug organizations. The Columbians left the smuggling risks to the Mexicans who pocketed additional profits.[98]

The Mexican drug organizations have also expanded their smuggling efforts within the borders of the United States. "Traffickers typically transport drug shipments to various urban venues ... and turn the shipments over to ... distribution networks ... Major hub cities for trafficking groups include Chicago New York City, Los Angeles and Houston."[99]

But before the drugs can get to the eager consumers in American cities, they have to cross the border. Let's look at an example - the exploits of one Rafael Munoz Talavera, in 1988. Munoz hooked up with the two Columbian drug cartels, the Medellin and Cali cartels. He moved a quarter million kilos (550,000 pounds) to El Paso, Texas, driving it across the border in automobiles. He never got caught. A few of the oft-lauded American border patrol agents made sure that the cars came through unscathed. They were handsomely rewarded.[100]

Illegal imports came across other parts of the border as well. "Asian DTOs [Drug Trafficking Organizations] and criminal groups based in Canada have emerged as significant ... distributors of ... marijuana and MDMA [ecstasy] to ... the United States." Just like with Alcohol prohibition, the northern border leaks contraband into the forty-eight states to the south. "Columbian, Dominican, Cuban and Jamaican DTOs [also] serve as major transporters and distributors of illicit drugs in the United States." The Dominicans bring in cocaine and heroin while the Jamaicans specialize in marijuana, maan. Whatever the product, the smuggling routes of the Prohibition era have been reestablished in the drug era.[101]

And while the product has changed, the propensity of smugglers to employ unique importation techniques has not. Smugglers have snuck illegal drugs into the United States in a "gas tank, or statue ... engines and children's electronic games." Inspectors in Miami x-rayed butter cans and found 72 kilos of cocaine. California inspectors found 315 kilos of marijuana in decorative rocks. Passengers, often paid by smugglers, put product in their luggage, their clothes and inside their bodies (don't ask!).[102]

"Importers" also used more traditional methods of entry - cars, trucks and even snowmobiles. And as with the bootleggers of the 20s and 30s, smugglers floated boats, from canoes to cruise ships, to move their merchandise. They also flew every type of aircraft available, commercial and private. They even sent drugs via express mail services and the internet. I am not sure if you get free shipping with large orders or not.[103]

DRUG ORGANIZATIONS

The sale of drugs has created very large criminal organizations that threaten their own countries and lay siege to America as well. American cities are infected by street gangs who also survive, in a large part, on the sale of drugs. If we stop their drug sales, we will stop their existence as well. But as they do currently exist, a sample of those existing organizations is our next topic.

THE COLUMBIAN
CARTELS

Just as the Mafia grew out of the banning of booze, illegal drug suppliers have grown out of the prohibition on drugs. Drug Cartels are one of the most evil of those supply groups. In Columbia, two of the most powerful were the Medellin and the Cali cartels. In Mexico, several cartels have been historically active. [104]

In 1975, an up and coming crook named Pablo Escobar took over the reins of a Columbian drug gang. Escobar eventually turned that enterprise into a multibillion dollar business known as the Medellin Cartel, named for the city in which it was based. At its peak, the cartel controlled some 80% of the cocaine that entered the United States. Some estimates have the cartel earning as much as $30 billion annually. Escobar used the money to buy vehicles, for the land, sea and air, as well as to fund his own band of mercenaries. The guy even bought a couple small submarines for smuggling coke. But before he did all that, he and some drug buddies got popped coming back from a "business" trip to Ecuador.[105]

That business trip was the genesis of the business model that Escobar adopted. That model was called "plato o plomo", Spanish for silver or lead. That is, Escobar controlled his kingdom by either filling his antagonists' wallets with cash or filling their bodies with bullets.[106]

Escobar tried to bribe his way out of the charges. When that didn't work, he killed the arresting officers. Case dismissed. The process worked so well that Escobar used it over and over. He bribed judges and politicians. Some took the money and some did not. Many of those who did not, felt the fatal wrath of Escobar. The number of deaths is believed to be in the hundreds. In one case, Escobar was meeting with one George Jung. According to Jung, a person was delivered to Escobar by two bodyguards. Escobar excused himself and went and killed the man. On returning to Jung, Escobar explained that the man had turned on Escobar.[107]

Escobar got his on December 2, 1992. He had been on the run for over a year after escaping from prison. He was finally located by a trace of a telephone call that he made. He was shot down on the roof of the building as he tried to escape. That was the end of the Medellin Cartel but not the end of the problem. Escobar's rival, the Cali Cartel remained in business.[108]

The Cali Cartel, which like the Medellin Cartel was named for its Columbian location, was the brainchild of the two Orejuela brothers and Santacruz Londono. The boys put together an empire similar to Pablo Escobar's. They smuggled cocaine, eventually capturing the same 80% of the trade that the Medellin Cartel had controlled.

U.S. Attorney General Alberto Gonzales laid out the extent of their cocaine import business - over 200 tons in a "score" of years (that's twenty – see the Gettysburg Address). To accomplish this business success, they bribed politicians. Some say even the former president, Ernesto Samper, received contributions from the cartel's coffers.[109]

However, the Cali Cartel was not as in your face as the Medellin Cartel had been. They put their profits into legitimate businesses. They hired attorneys to scout the activities of the DEA. They employed electrical geeks to design communications systems that competitors (and the rare enforcement official) could not bug. But their level of sophistication does not mean that they weren't violent.[110]

The members of the Cali Cartel were mortal enemies of Pablo Escobar. They even formed Los Pepes – People against Pablo Escobar. I shouldn't laugh, but that really is funny. At any rate, as Escobar got more violent, Los Pepes fought back. During the war between the two cartels, hundreds of people died. In addition to the criminals, many members of the justice system perished.[111]

Eventually, the brothers were caught. In the 1990s, they got prison sentences of up to 15 years. There is some speculation that they continued to run the store from inside the big house.[112]

THE MEXICAN CARTELS

No big house horseplay for the Mexican cartels. The Mexicans seem to run their businesses, drug sales key among them, wherever they like. Those cartels include the Gulf, Sinaloa and Juarez cartels as well as a very active Tijuana cartel. Turf wars among those entities have escalated as time has passed. Complicating an already degenerating situation, government officials, from street cops to drug czars, are often are involved with the sale of drugs by the cartels. Most alarmingly, violence from the sale of those drugs is slowly seeping into the United States. [113]

That violence is a byproduct of the sale of the Cartels' main product – drugs. The Mexican cartels supply marijuana and methamphetamine to the United States. They also ship heroin to American addicts from their bases south of the border. The cartels grow the marijuana and the poppies right at home in Mexico. They also manufacture the Meth in country. Hecho en Mexico! However, they import their cocaine from South America.

As of 2007, some 90% of the coke that slips into the states came through Mexico.[114]

The Gulf Cartel is one of the big boys. So big, in fact, that they have their own army - the Zetas. The Zetas began with about 30 ex-Mex military. They have since recruited policemen, military and local thugs to round out the troops. They are so powerful that they can openly advertise for help. In one case, they hung help wanted ads on highway overpasses. The ads offered top pay and *benefits*![115]

The Zetas are capable of sophisticated operations in which they employ military weapons like submachine guns and small rockets. They have set up training camps in Mexico to bring their horde of evil ogres up to speed. With that training, the gangsters can carry out the kidnapping, torture and beheadings that have become so common today.[116]

So common, in fact, that they are regularly featured in newspapers and television in the United States. On September 17th, 2008, The Daily News (Los Angeles) reported that eight people were killed and ten times that were injured when druggies pitched a couple of grenades into a crowd of people celebrating Mexico's Independence Day. On November 11th, the same paper reported that seven more were killed in Juarez. One man was decapitated, his hands were cut off and then he was burned. Two weeks later, another report from that publication said that another seven bodies had been found. A competing gang had beaten them up and then gunned them down. Three messages were left by the bodies as a warning to the offending gang.[117]

One of those rival gangs is the Sinaloa Cartel. This cartel runs deep and long. The roots of its supplies wander all the way back to the 19th century. At that time, the agricultural region of Mexico that would eventually spawn these killers was being used to grow opium for the Chinese immigrants who had come to the new world. They brought some old world habits with them and opium was one of the biggest. Opium production got much bigger in the 20th century. For one thing, the United States government needed morphine for its troops during World War II. They had it grown, gladly, by the farmers in ole Mexico. The American government ceased its importation of opium after the war but the Mexican farmers kept sending it anyway. They just needed a little help from the drug lords.[118]

And key among those drug lords were the jefes of the Sinaloa Cartel. By the middle of the century, they were buying up the local pot and poppies and shipping them off to beatniks and hippies in the upper forty-eight. Come the eighties, they hooked up with the Columbian Cartels. The Columbians were having trouble getting their product across the border. They subcontracted the Sinaloa Cartel to provide that service. In time, the Sinaloa Cartel demanded payment for those services in coke instead of cash. That allowed the Mexicans to get a much bigger piece of the pie, by exporting their share of the drugs into the bottomless pit of consumption in America[119].

To protect their growing enterprise, the Sinaloa Cartel also recruited an army. Their armies are called the Negros and the Pelones. They are not as sophisticated as the Zetas but they are just as effective in carrying on turf wars against the other Cartels. Part of the city of

Culiacan, the capital city of the state of Sinaloa, has had so much gunplay that it has been compared to Chicago, Al Capone's late kingdom. The legacy of the bootleggers lives on.[120]

The drug cartels live on as well. A shining example of that is the Tijuana Cartel. This group of gangsters is responsible for drug traffic in the tons: including marijuana, cocaine, methamphetamine and heroin. In order to keep the drugs flowing without government interference, they donated in the order of $1,000,000 a WEEK (in 1997), to the local authorities. To avoid roadblocks from rivals (and uncooperative law enforcement officials), they, like all good gangsters, employ their own military, armed and dangerous. If you get in their way, you get dead.[121]

And an awful lot of people are getting dead. Five beaten bodies were found by a shopping center. The bodies of two men whose heads were cut off were found by a city road. Their heads were found elsewhere, wrapped in bags. Four children were killed as collateral damage in a gang shootout. The family members of a rival gang were kidnapped. The children were thrown off a bridge and a videotape of the crime was sent to the rival. At the same time, the man received the head of his wife. The Arellano brothers (since captured and/or killed) conducted human barbecues. This consisted of roasting dads, moms and their children, above burning rubber tires. *The Los Angeles Times* reported in October, 2008 that twelve corpses were found near a grade school. Some had their tongues intact, others did not.[122]

In 2010, the violence escalated beyond even that evil. Six people were gunned down in a saloon in Mazatlan, putting to rest the oft held California tourist belief that "you're pretty safe in the big tourist towns." In El Porvenir, Mexico, the cartels had begun burning down houses and leaving warning notes that instructed the residents to leave before they were killed. Apparently, the town was inconveniently located in the path of the drug trade.[123]

The list goes on and on, and from all over Mexico, not just Tijuana. Examples are in the paper weekly and on the tube whenever they are particularly heinous (like the killing of Cardinal Posadas Ocampo at the Guadalajara airport). The point is that people are being killed in droves. The Daily News reported that in 2007, gangland killings totaled 2,477. The figure for January through November of 2008 had risen to 5,376! The BBC, quoting Mexican newspaper *El Universal* in a report on 12/4/2008, wrote that, for over a month, an average of 24 people had been killed each day – una por hora![124]

And they're not just killing civilians. National and local drug enforcement officials are living in fear for their lives as well. The Daily News reported on 12/17/08, that hit men had injured three agents when they shot up the State Attorney General's facility in Tijuana. The Interior Secretary, Juan Camilo Mourino, who was an advisor of the Mexican president, was the victim of a mysterious, sudden plane crash in November, 2008. In another report, the discovery of a note listing 26 targeted policemen was followed by the subsequent discovery of a police commandant who had been gunned down. So, these creeps aren't just killing randomly as the situation requires, they're making a list and checking it twice. Naughty and not Nice.[125]

And the hits just keep coming. On 12/21/08, nine more headless bodies were found in Guerrero, some of whom were soldiers. A note was found that basically said – you kill one, I'll kill ten. More recently, in April, 2010, the cartels attacked the army in seven separate incidents. The cartel actually blocked the road and fired on the soldiers. The soldiers prevailed and, while doing so, captured military style weapons and transports. However, these direct attacks on the military are a very disturbing move toward total anarchy in Mexico. And all of it due to the illegal sales of drugs.[126]

These killers are unstoppable, as long as they have the enormous financial resources that the sale of illegal drugs provides. Those two fundamental tools, murder and money, contribute to the corruption that is rampant in Mexico. The cartels can kill you if they want to. They can kill the people that you love if they want to. Alternatively, you can take their bribes, look the other way and live to love another day. Of course, you could always quit your job, but that is no guarantee that you won't be killed anyway, just because of what you know.

As a result, corruption permeates the entire country of Mexico. The BBC News wrote that the facts clearly show that the many of the Mexican authorities are working with the cartels. Some of that evidence follows. In August, 2008, Carlos Cepano Filippini, a federal police commander, was arrested and charged with banking $500,000 in drug profits. Three months later, a former Federal employee named Rodolfo de la Guardia Garcia, was busted for giving information to the Sinaloa Cartel. Not to be outdone, another Fed, Noe Ramirez, faced charges that he, too, took $500,000 from the Cartels.[127]

But it isn't just individual "high" ranking dudes that are taking the cartel cash. In 2005, about 20% of the 7000 agents in AFI (the Federal Investigative Agency) were investigated and 457 of them were charged with crimes. In Neuvo Laredo, local cops shot at Federal agents. Forty-one local cops were arrested. In Nuevo Leon, 100 plus agents were suspended in connection with corruption.[128]

The Mexican problem is affecting other countries as well. Interpol has had to extend its prodigious reach into Mexico. After another police official was arrested, the legendary international policing organization, sent agents to Mexico to see if some of their data had been given to the cartels as well.[129]

As Interpol had surmised, the evil had spread beyond Mexico's borders. More to our point, it had swept across the Rio Grande like a giant, swarming band of bandidos. American cities are feeling the infection of this festering sore from the south. In Southern California, a tunnel was found that ran from Tijuana to San Diego. It is possible that the tunnel was to be used to bring donations from Mexico to America's homeless but I suspect that a more nefarious intention existed. In San Antonio, Texas, Gabriel Jalomo Rodriguez, who sure seemed to be a hit man was arrested. In Starr County, in Texas, County Sheriff Reymundo Guerra was arrested on charges of drug smuggling. A little ways north, near Reno, Nevada, "The biggest little city in the world," three biologists found themselves staring at pistols in the hands of cartel members. The unsuspecting scientists had stumbled upon a pot field that was guarded by gangsters. The biologists were eventually released. They were lucky, muy lucky. The Mexican cartels have been growing pot in California National Parks more frequently. Some fields have yields of nearly a hundred thousand pounds of pot a year. The cartels have often guarded these gold mines with thugs armed with AK-47s. Stumbling upon a illicit field could definitely ruin your backpacking trip. In addition to growing weed in the wilderness, the cartels are cultivating a growing business relationship with street gangs in U.S. cities. However, we will look at that bit of bad news later on in this chapter.[130]

But before that, we will take a quick look at other effects of the drug war on Americans. The number one effect is that Americans are dying. And not drug users, innocent bystanders. In Ciudad Juarez, in March, 2010, an employee of the U.S. consulate, Leslie Enriquez and her spouse, Arthur Redelfs, were killed by gunman. A teenager in El Paso, Texas, Tania Lozya , was killed by a bullet that was fired by a gunman chasing another man through the backyard at her aunt's house. A principal of a California school, Augustin Salcedo, was taken from a restaurant with five other men. They were all murdered. Salcedo was simply in the wrong place at the wrong time. And he was not alone. The Daily News reported on March 21, 2010 that the number of Americans killed in Mexico was twice as many in 2009 as 2007 - seventy-nine.[131]

TERRORISTS

Guess what the terrorists do to help fund *their* murderous plans? Did you say sell drugs? That is entirely correct. The Taliban, their protected terrorist friend Osama Bin Laden, FARC and others sell opium, cocaine, etc., to drug users in Europe and America. They use the profits from the drug sales to buy weapons to kill those same Europeans and Americans.

Ninety-five percent of the world's supply of one of the most powerful of those drugs, opium, is grown in Afghanistan. The Taliban, both while they were in power in Afghanistan and in an attempt to retake the country, have supported the cultivation of the poppy by the nation's farmers. The Taliban then places a 10% tax on the opium and heroin that comes from the plants. The Taliban have profited tremendously from the sale of that opium for years. The financial windfall collected by the Taliban was estimated to be from 375 to 800 million dollars per year when they were in power. Despite their removal from power, the Taliban continues its presence in Afghanistan and still earns 60 to 80 million dollars per year. A State

Department official noted that big armies are only a big bank account away.[132]

The Taliban's terrorist army is spreading out. In 2008, it retook a good deal of Afghanistan. By the end of the year, the Taliban began to take some of Pakistan as well. The Daily News reported that the Swat valley, in Pakistan, was controlled by the Taliban. The Swat valley continued to be a problem for Pakistan in 2009 as well.[133]

The Taliban uses the proceeds from opium sales to fund their military and political terrorist activities. That's where Osama bin Laden comes in. His Al-Qaida terrorist organization, one of the world's most dangerous, is also funded by drug sales (apparently for this "devout" Muslim, feeding pork to his family is a sin but feeding heroin to teenagers is not). Anyway, along with the drug money, the Taliban, when they were in power, allowed Al-Qaeda to live and train its troops in Afghanistan. Osama bin Laden's gang of killers gained strength and legitimacy via the sale of drugs. Legalized drugs would have provided no help whatsoever to these evil war mongers.[134]

Other warring organizations around the globe exploit the drug market in order to pay their bills too. In Columbia, three competing organizations have used drug money to help finance their revolutionary activities. Those three entities were the Revolutionary Armed Forces of Columbia (FARC), The National Liberation Army (ELN) and the United Self-Defense Groups of Columbia (AUC).[135]

The first of these, the FARC, has been in the revolution business in Columbia since the sixties. And along the way, it has been designated a terrorist organization by the United States. FARC has earned that moniker. It is guilty of kidnapping hundreds of people, in order to fund itself. In 2001, FARC kidnapped and killed a former government official. In November, 2005, they kidnapped sixty people. One of its most famous abductions was that of Ingrid Betancourt, a presidential candidate. She was freed in 2008 when Columbian soldiers, posing as friends of FARC, tricked her captors into releasing her. They are still holding hundreds of hostages today.[136]

FARC is more than just kidnappers. They are murderers, hijackers and, of course, drug dealers. In 1999, they killed three U.S. missionaries. In 2002, they hijacked an airliner and captured a Columbian Senator. And to finance these activities, OF COURSE, they deal drugs. Fifty percent of their operating capital comes from the sale of drugs. FARC alleviates a large part of the world's lust for coke. The drug money is essential. It allows FARC to pay its soldiers and to buy the weapons with which they control their arena.[137]

Among the other Columbian cartels, ELN has some aversion to drug sales, the AUC is actively involved with them. It is estimated that up to seventy percent of AUC's operating cash comes from the drug trade. The AUC considers the sale of drugs to be morally wrong but logistically required. In November, 2002, an indictment was handed down in Houston against four men. They tried to buy equipment to help wage the AUC's war: missiles, grenades, rifles, pistols and ammunition. They came to the table with $25 million worth of drugs and money.[138]

Worldwide, insurgent groups use drug money to carry on violent uprisings against the governments where they reside. For example, in Peru, the Shining Path, a communist revolutionary group that began in the sixties, is dedicated to the overthrow of the Peruvian government. Over the years, they have managed to kill thousands of civilians. One report said that these killers saved bullets by killing its victims with machetes! These animals help fill their coffers by providing protection for local coca farmers as well as manufacturing cocaine themselves.[139]

Other terrorist organizations have taken advantage of the western world's continuing demand for non-alcoholic intoxicants. The DEA found that part of the money collected by meth rings were going to Hezbollah, an organization that the US has declared to be terrorists. Elsewhere in the region, drug profits in Afghanistan have been routed to the bank accounts of the Islamic Movement of Uzbekistan (IMU). Speed freaks and crack heads are helping heat up the Middle East. The sale of these drugs help terrorists kill American servicemen and women as well as innocent people. As a result, each year we get more Middle East Muddle, pushed forward by terrorist drug pushers.[140]

GANGS

Here at home, American drug pushers are a significant problem as well. Uppermost among those street druggists are the hordes of gang members in large metropolitan areas throughout the country. Three gangs of particular note are the Crips, Bloods and the MS-13 gang.

The Crips are a drug selling, murdering, criminal gang that started up in Los Angeles, California late in the 1960s. They wear the color blue. They replace the letter "b" in any word with a "c" to disrespect their rivals, the Bloods. Despite these childish traits, they are an extremely violent gang which has spread across the whole United States.[141]

And the Crips have been active in many of those States. On September 28, 2007, a federal racketeering case was filed against ten members of the Crips in Kansas. No, really, Kansas. They sported nicknames like "Insane Tommy" and "nut case." Truth in advertising, I love it! These criminals were charged with "attempting to use violence … to … expand the power of the Crips … and to protect their criminal enterprise from interference by law enforcement." The case noted "a criminal enterprise in which murder [four murders and eleven attempted murders], drive-by shootings, robbery and drug trafficking crimes were treated as tools for doing business." These were not nice people. And, of course, they sold drugs (the indictment specifically mentioned cocaine, crack cocaine and marijuana) to help keep their boat afloat.[142]

Trying to sink that boat would be their rival gang, the Bloods. They also began their trip to hell in Southern California. But these guys are way different. First, they wear the color red! Second, they cross out the letter "c" in words to disrespect the Crips. However, like the Crips, they are vicious, drug dealing, murdering criminals.[143]

For example, ten gangsters from a Blood gang in Las Vegas called the Playboy Bloods (I could not possibly make that name up!) were indicted on charges that they "committed acts of violence and drug trafficking [as well as] Use of a Firearm During a Crime of Violence." These choirboys had less meaningful nicknames than the Crips, basically just using their first name and an initial. I'm afraid that they lose points on the nicknames. But the logo is inspired: a Playboy Bunny. Points awarded.[144]

However, these bunny boys were anything but cute and cuddly. They were accused of murdering a security guard, shooting him in the back as he bicycled away. They were also accused of killing one Billy Thomas, also shot in the back. And they financed these activities with the money they made selling crack. [145]

Drug sales also help support another gang, the MS-13. In addition, they engage in car theft, burglary, gun sales, and assault. Rape and extortion are also listed on these guys' business cards.[146]

Of course, gangsters have their own sort of business cards. The 10,000 American gang bangers and the 50,000 South American members often sport visible IDs. These ID cards are actually body art: an elaborate "13" or an "M", [the 13th letter of the alphabet], or "MS". [147]

MS-13 was begun by immigrants from El Salvador who were fleeing that country's civil war in the 1980s. They still have a presence in El Salvador as well as in a couple other Central American countries and, surprise, Mexico.[148]

MS-13 is particularly vicious, mastering a number of different weapons. In Houston, in 2005, MS-13 members staged a paramilitary attack on a rival gang's house that was a storage point for drugs. They used lookouts and an AK-47 to conduct a search of the house with the professionalism of a swat team. When the authorities arrived, a shootout commenced in which two gangsters were killed and four arrested. When they're not using high tech rifles, these killers sometimes, going it old school, unsheathe their machetes. In one case, the head of a female officer was cut so severely that she was nearly decapitated. In a separate case, an opposing gang member had a few fingers chopped off with a machete.[149]

When these guys aren't reverting to barbarianism, they can actually be creative little criminals. In 2005, in Madison, Wisconsin, MS-13 gangsters were arrested after stealing about $50,000 worth of over the counter drugs at different Walgreen stores. They used some of the stolen medicines to manufacture drugs and shipped the rest to Louisville to be resold. These guys were sophisticated criminals. In order to steal the medicine, they employed lined bags that resisted the beepers used by retailers to prevent stolen goods from "walking out the door."[150]

In addition to these sophisticated and creative thugs, thousands of smaller gangs cause havoc all across America, fueled, of course, by drug sales. The Daily News wrote that gangs sold drugs to earn money to run their organizations. Warfare inevitably began between those gangs, based on each gang's desire to keep the profits of their turf for themselves. The following are random stories about violence related to these murderous vermin that I pulled from the Daily News as well as the internet.[151]

Francisco Zambrano, a member of the Vineland Boys, a gang in the Los Angeles area, was found guilty of the attempted murder of a Marine named Bryan Guerra. Mister Guerra's offense? Apparently, he had "disrespected" Zamboro. Other members of the gang kill people as well. Vineland Boys were implicated in four other killings, one of which was the murder of Matthew Pavelka, a member of the Burbank police force.[152]

Downtown Los Angeles, around MacArthur Park, is the turf of another band of thugs, the 18th street gang. On October 25, 2007, 18 members (coincidence?) were arrested for violence. The tuff-guy tactics used by the 18th street gang were intended to protect the gang's sale of coke in the park. The gangsters were arrested for drug sales and illegal gun sales. Residents also reported 23 complaints of extortion around the park. On September 16, 2007, gang members were suspected of shooting at a local vendor. One of the bullets struck and killed a baby boy. You will note that it is the drug money that keeps these clowns in business.[153]

Another group of violent, drug-selling thugs is a motorcycle club called the Mongols. They are the enemies of the Hell's Angels. They were formed because the Hell's Angels would not allow Hispanic men to join their club. The two clubs made headlines on April 27, 2002, during the annual motorcycle ride called the River Run in Laughlin, Nevada. The Mongols entered Harrah's casino and began a confrontation with the Hell's Angels, who were already at the casino. A shootout began between the two gangs right on the casino floor. Patrons hit the floor in panic. In the end, three gang members died and another thirteen were wounded. Fortunately, no one from the general public was injured.[154]

In 2008, 60 members of the murdering Mongols were arrested for drugs, guns and murder. Individual Mongol arrests include Peter Soto, arrested in 2006 for selling meth, Abe Wedig for assaulting a black man in Hollywood and Shawn Buss, who was accused of helping Abe with the undoubtedly racially motivated crime. Oh yeah, these last two were also accused of selling drugs. Who'd a thunk it?[155]

But not all the violence can be attributed to a particular gang. Often, reports of violence simply note that the shootings are "gang related." In Central City, California, in January, 2009, a 6-year-old girl was shot in the back by a stray bullet that entered her home. It was simply listed as gang related. The next day, she was listed in stable condition. She survived, but other innocent bystanders have not. The accidental shooting of children by gangsters is an all too frequent occurrence. That same month saw an even more tragic murder. A family of four were told to kneel by the side of a Florida Turnpike. Two gang members were apparently settling a score with the father of the family, Jose Luis Escodedo. Jose was shot to death along with his wife Yessica, who was gunned down while holding her two sons, ages three and four. The report in the Daily News said that the killings were part of an ongoing war among rival members of the *same* coke ring. [156]

The National Drug Intelligence Center released an assessment of the gang problem in 2006. In it, referring to gangs, the Center noted that "their involvement in drug activity continue [sic] to increase throughout the country." The gangs have evolved from street punks to "sophisticated, profit-driven, organized criminal enterprises that engage in polydrug trafficking." Those drugs include: "cocaine, heroin, marijuana and methamphetamine." And along with the drug sales comes the need to protect the gang's turf. The report says that the threat to society "is magnified by the high and increasing level of violence associated with expansion of drug trafficking activities by gangs." The issue facing our society is not only drug sales but the killings and other criminal activities that those drug sales support.[157]

Gangs commit many different crimes. Burglary, bank robbery, extortion, illegal sales of weapons, credit card fraud, rape and murder (including, but not limited to drive-by shootings) are all activities in which gangs are involved. Some gangs excel at robbery, some at extortion. But almost all of them sell drugs. The huge profits generated by the sale of drugs help pay the gang's cost of business, including the paychecks of its members. Cut out the drug sales and you cut out the heart of the gang.

CORRUPTION

Just as we saw during the Prohibition era, the war on drugs has spurred a significant rise in corruption among government officials. As the General Accounting Office reported way back in 1998, "Investigations of drug-related police corruption found on-duty police officers engaged in serious criminal activities, such as ... stealing money and/or drugs from drug dealers ... selling stolen drugs [and]... protecting drug operations." Although I would not be surprised to discover other government employees who were involved in drug sales in some manner, the following is a list, in alphabetical order, of those entities in which I found indicted employees. There is evidence against members of the Air Force and the Army, as well as officers and agents of the California Highway Patrol, Customs and Border Protection, the Immigration and Naturalization Services, Jail guards, National Guardsmen, various Police officers, Prison guards, Sheriffs, Sheriff's deputies and State Policemen. We are only going to look at a few of these but rest assured, they all exist and there are plenty more where those came from.[158]

Let's look at the servicemen first. Now, don't get me wrong. I have tremendous respect for the young American servicemen and women who put their lives on the line for our freedoms. The members of the military who appear here, however, are not heroes. Quite the opposite, they are villains. They took advantage of their unique position to cheat the American people while personally enriching themselves.

First up is Army Staff Sergeant Irizarry-Melendez. In September, 2005, the good sergeant entered a guilty plea to bringing in coke and cash from Columbia. As part of his job, Sgt. Irizarry-Melendez was assigned the duties of coordinating substance abuse work in his unit. One of his compadres, Spc. Francisco Rosa, also admitted that he was involved with drugs. He got five years in prison. A third soldier was also implicated in the case.[159]

A much larger group of criminals, sixteen Federal employees, was reported by the Los Angeles Times on May 13, 2005. The group included members of the Army, the US Bureau of Prisons, and the Immigration Service in addition to various Arizona state and local enforcement agencies. All pleaded guilty to moving over 1,200 pounds of coke and picking up $222,000. They committed these crimes while in uniform and in official government vehicles.[160]

Another American "drug cartel" was composed mostly of cops and Arizona National Guardsmen. There were over fifty of them involved. One of these was a former sergeant in the Air Force, Rommel Schroer. He admitted to taking a bribe from an FBI agent (he went to the big house for $7,500!), moving some 30 kilos of coke and extortion. This guy and his co-conspirators disgraced their uniforms.[161]

Law enforcement officials also disgraced their uniforms. One such case took place in Albuquerque, New Mexico. The date was December 11, 2008. Ex-State Police Officer Keith Salazar and Sheriff's Deputy Levi Countryman were convicted (they pleaded guilty) of drug charges. Court papers also reported that drug dealers bribed the pair to provide law enforcement data to the dealers. Nice guys. They got six years each. In Santa Ana, California, just down road from where I am sitting as I write this, an Ex-California Highway Patrolman, Joshua Blackburn, got almost six years as well. He was found guilty of burglary and cocaine possession (88 pounds).[162]

Coke was also the drug of choice for an ex-police officer from Chicago. Joseph Miedzianowski was convicted of selling cocaine from Chicago to Miami, Florida. He was sentenced to life in prison. The judge in the case, Judge Blanche Manning, said that Miedzianowski had turned his back on the people that he had sworn "to protect and to serve" by selling drugs and providing weapons to gangsters.[163]

But cocaine is not the only drug that our police are selling to the populace. A dismissed Massachusetts state trooper, Mark Lemieux, who was arrested in 2007, entered a guilty plea in a Boston court. He admitted to helping to provide Oxycontin. He also extorted customers to get delinquent payments.[164]

Collecting drug money was also one of the specialties of Rafael Pacheco, Jr., a former Special Agent who worked for the US Customs Service. Mr. Pacheco was guilty of taking bribes in 2005. Twenty-seven of them. He took some $25,000 in bribes from one Fidencio Estrada, whom he understood was a drug pusher. But Pacheco didn't limit himself to one offense. He captured data about Estrada from federal databases and shared those data with the drug trafficker. He issued a letter to the American Consulate in Monterey, Mexico that claimed that Mr. Estrada was working for the US Customs Service. Despite these obvious attempts to cover his tracks, Pacheco was busted after his business card was found in Estrada's car during a traffic stop. Amazing! Pacheco actually gave his business card to his criminal accomplice. No chance of something going wrong there![165]

Within a year, something definitely went wrong for our second contestant. In 2006, Lizandro Martinez admitted to trafficking in drugs and laundering money. In his 14 years with the Customs Service, Martinez filled his pockets with about $750,000. He was paid $10,000 a truckload for allowing drug traffickers to drive from Mexico, unmolested, through his lane at the Progreso International Bridge in Texas.[166]

But the corruption isn't limited to the west coast. Our final contestant comes to us from Miami, Florida. After working only three months for Customs and Border Protection, Edwin Disla was found guilty in 2008 in a case involving heroin and coke. Authorities ran a sting on Disla in which he smuggled fake heroin and cocaine out of Puerto Rico and into Miami. He used his status as a Customs Agent to facilitate his odious undertaking. He was arrested in March, 2007, in Puerto Rico after receiving 25 kilograms of fake junk.[167]

Although I have just spent more than three pages listing cases of malfeasance, I do not mean to imply that these pearls of US law enforcement are the norm. I believe that the preponderance of policing agencies is staffed with, honest, hard working agents. On the other hand, as we all know, criminal convictions represent only the tip of the iceberg of the total number of any type of crime that is committed annually in this country. For example, how many times have you, yourself, been guilty of speeding? How many times have you been caught? Exactly. Nonetheless, whenever authorities prohibit a highly demanded product, some of the officers whose task it is to enforce the ban will see the potential to afford a sports car or speedboat and will be willing to take the risks.

THE PRODUCT

American consumers are protected from legal products that can harm them, tobacco being a notable exception, by various government agencies. Among others, those agencies include the Food and Drug Administration (FDA), the Food Safety and Inspection Service (FSIS) and the Centers for Disease Control and Prevention (CDC). No such agencies exist for the safe dispensation of illegal drugs. The consumer is on his own to determine if the product that he is swallowing, snorting or shooting is safe. That is a precarious position at best. In order to improve profits, dealers often cut their products with other substances, thereby increasing the quantity of product while decreasing its quality. We saw the exact same phenomenon during Prohibition. And as was true in that period, the "cutters" of today sometimes bulk up their product with substitute chemicals that are harmful, even deadly. They can do this without fear of consequences. What is the consumer to do? Are they to call the FDA and complain that the cocaine they have in their possession is not pure? Should they report that they almost died in the emergency room last night because the heroin that they shot up had been adulterated? Not gonna happen. The report, that is; the emergency room visits will most certainly continue. [168]

Those medical problems are often a consequence of ingesting unknown contaminants along with the drug of choice. Marijuana is an interesting example. All kinds of chemicals are mixed in with the evil weed, sometimes to increase the high but much more often to increase the high profits.

Additionally complicating factors for the consumer are the different levels of quality of an ounce of herb and the prices associated with the sale. There are different levels of quality of pot and the salesmen can mix some of the lower quality pot in with some of the higher quality pot in order to increase their profits. The consumer, unaware of the degraded condition of the marijuana can end up paying penthouse prices for basement dwelling weed. Again, the consumer has no governmental protection against this.

Like the butcher with his thumb on the scale, drug suppliers routinely beef up the quantity of their product to get extra profit. In Europe, pushers have found incredible ways to pad their pot: adding glass beads to marijuana in Holland and sneaking in lead to some grass in Germany. It is noteworthy that the additional weight of the lead could add as much as $1,500 of pure profit to a kilogram of marijuana.[169]

The list of possible contaminants is endless. Some are filler and some fatal. Here, we will list a few of them to illustrate the breadth of the list. Adulterants found mixed in with marijuana include PCP, cocaine, embalming fluid (I'm not making this up), cement and soap. The list is longer than that but I think you get the idea. Consumers are being cheated and, in some cases, killed by this unregulated process.[170]

In contrast with the lack of regulation of adulterants that are mixed into weed, the quality and price of the pot itself *is* somewhat regulated by the market. The prices listed here, which are based on the quality of the weed, are from 2006. The quality, and therefore the price, is base on three distinct categories of weed (some publications use more categories but, for our purposes, three will do). However, before we begin, let me be clear- there is no regulating agency to ensure that the following categories are clearly delineated. In order to maximize profits, the mixing of lower categories into higher categories by unscrupulous criminals can virtually be guaranteed.[171]

The first category is the lowest. It is commonly called schwag. Schwag is brown, dry and loaded with seeds. Seeds in pot are a bad thing. Schwag was selling for about $100 an ounce in 2006. The second category is the mids. These buds are generally more moist than the schwag. This class of grass will set you back about $150 an ounce. Pot heads like this category a lot. The top tier is called high-quality. This marijuana has hairs (red or white) and crystals on the weed. This category produces an intoxicant effect in the head. Lower tier pot has a stronger effect on the torso than the cranium. The good stuff goes for about $250 an ounce.[172]

Another pricey intoxicant is the ever popular nose candy, cocaine. And the Kings of cocaine, not to be outdone by the pot pushers, are equally happy to introduce various powders into their product to increase their ill-gotten gains. As we have seen during Prohibition in the thirties and more recently with the adulteration of Marijuana, these unregulated and, at least originally, untested contaminants cost the consumer dearly, whether taking their money or leaving them in the morgue.

Interestingly, this contamination of product is not a new problem. The New York Times printed a story, originally reported in the St. Louis Globe-Democrat, that investigated this very issue. To determine if the cocaine that they had on hand had been altered, pharmacists had ordered a drug analysis to be conducted by some scientists in the East. The report that came back showed that up to 75% of the powder was borax and that only a small amount of cocaine was contained in the mixture. This article was first printed in the New York Times on December 11, 1887. Yes, *that* 1887. Some one hundred and twenty years ago. This unregulated profit taking has been going on a long time indeed.[173]

But we are interested in the profiteers of the 21st century. Sadly, the situation has not improved. Cocaine is still cut with foreign substances at a very high level. Common chemicals added to cocaine are many: phenacetin, which is for combating pain but has been banned in select locations. Also used as additives are three dental drugs: lignocaine, benzocaine and procaine. These three contaminants, discovered in tests in Ireland, are interesting because of their numbing effect. Pure cocaine numbs the user's gums when rubbed against them, thereby creating a simple test for the purity of the drug. A prospective buyer can rub some coke on his gums. If his gums go numb, the powder is coke. The dental drugs listed above do the same thing and so they pass the numbness test. The buyer is cheated and, infinitely more importantly, possibly endangered, by the lack of consumer protection in the sale of black market drugs.[174]

Taking full advantage of that lack of protection, drug traffickers have cut their coke with other products as well. High percentages of cocaine samples collected in Slovenia contained some of these additives. The added substances included sugars, caffeine and lidocaine, with a contaminant range of from a low of 22% to a high of over 60%. Another contaminant, reported in Vancouver, Canada, was levamisole. Levamisole is used to treat pigs that have worms. In humans, it can cause infection, pneumonia, and painful sores among other nastiness, including potentially fatal episodes in persons who are allergic to it.[175]

The practice of cutting cocaine, and any other drug, can be fatal in another way as well. In addition to our century old example above, there is ample evidence of substantial adulteration of black market drugs today. The Slovenia research found "A purity of cocaine [that] ranged from 10.6% to 80.6%, with an average of 37%." Tests in Ireland found similar results. The coke that they examined "had purity levels of between 8 per cent and 77 percent, with most ... being in the 20 per cent to 35 per cent range." Those numbers are disturbing, to say the least. We can see that the average purity runs about 35 per cent. However, it could be double that. If a user is expecting 35 and is fed 70, he has unwittingly ingested twice as much cocaine as he had intended. Clearly, problems will arise and some of those problems will have to be dealt with by the deceased's next of kin.[176]

Problems with purity are not restricted to marijuana and cocaine. Every black market drug is a target for increased profits via decreased purity. The last one that we're going to look at, as I'm sure you've guessed by now, is heroin.

Heroin is mixed with all kinds of junk, just as with pot and coke. The Irish study found noscapine, which is for coughs, and papaverine, an anti-impotence treatment. In Chicago, heroin mixed with Fentanyl, a highly potent pain-killer, has been killing junkies. Other favorite product expanders (as found in New York City) are: caffeine, benzoczine, cocaine (why would a dealer waste this?), lidocaine, sodium bicarbonate and Thioridazine (for sour stomach), quinine (a malaria drug), and disodium ethylenediame tetraacetic (a chelating agent for metals). I don't know what chelating means but it cannot be a good thing to inject into one's veins. This is, of course, only a partial list of the powders that find their way into smack.[177]

The parallels continue. The percentage of pure heroin varies greatly from sale to sale. Again landing in Ireland, we fine that while junk can be anywhere from 15 to 65% pure, the purity of most of the heroin taken in drug busts is more like a quarter to a half. The user is getting one half to three-quarters of junk mixed in with their junk. Even more dangerous, ironically, is pure, unadulterated heroin. Occasionally, pure heroin hits the streets. The pure stupidity of this from a business standpoint is mind boggling. What successful business gives the customer twice as much product as its customers expect? The real problem, of course, is that the unsuspecting addict will inject twice as much heroin as he thinks he is taking. This can easily lead to an overdose, sometimes resulting in death. An example of this was a report in *perthnow,* from Australia. On March 7, 2009, the report told of 5 heroin users who were found unconscious and revived in one night. That was an unusually high total for Perth. The most likely cause was heroin that was stronger than usual.[178]

Whatever the issue: unreliable pricing, adulteration of injectable or snortable powders, or mixed up packets of pot, the problem remains: the user is on his own. There is no government agency or consumer advocate bureau to control prices or purity of the product. This lack of regulation is dangerous, even deadly, to millions of drug users in America, indeed the world over.

THE COST

As with alcohol prohibition, the cost of keeping drugs under (out of?) control is itself prohibitive. US citizens lose out in two ways. First, the druggies get the revenue from the sale of the drugs. The government coffers are cheated out of billions of dollars in sales taxes as criminals collect 100% of the wholesale and retail sales revenue for these high demand products. Those retail suppliers and their associated growers and manufacturers are also failing to pay any corporate taxes, doubling the hit to the US Treasury accounts. On the other side of the coin, the taxpayers have to pay through the nose to control cocaine, heroin, etc. And just as we saw in the 1920s, in order to enforce the regressive, repressive anti-drug laws of the United States, billions of taxpayer's dollars are required. Those dollars are used to pay for all aspects of criminalizing drugs, including: enforcement, prosecution, and incarceration, both on the Federal and local levels.

TAXES

But before we look at criminalization, let's first look at taxation. The tax implications of legalization are enormous. Let's start with street sales. The United Nations, in 2007, estimated the street value of the total drug use in the world at $322 billion. The United States' share of that figure is put at approximately $60 billion dollars, nearly 20 percent of the world's sales. One hundred per cent of the excise taxes related to that value is currently lost. Additionally, the suppliers who are growing and/or processing the herbal and chemical intoxicants that the gangs deliver to America citizens are doing so without paying any corporate taxes. Lastly, the income taxes that should be paid by the workers at those suppliers' businesses are currently lost to the State and Federal governments.[179]

The $60 billion sales figure for the United States is arbitrary at best. However, based on the method which I used to determine it, I suspect that, if anything, it is low. First, a report from England (the US is surprisingly tightlipped about this figure) lists the sales figures for the US at $60 billion. Second, the National Drug Intelligence

Center estimates that an average of some $28.5 billion in drug money goes out of the USA, south, to Central and South American. If that much stays here in the US as well, we are at $57 billion, which makes the $60 billion seem reasonable. Of course, we don't have actual sales receipts (drug users are notoriously bad record keepers) so we can't be sure. Interestingly, another report showed the sales figures for 1998 at $65 billion. One would expect the price to have risen over a decade but the global depression that began in 2007 would certainly have adversely affected sales figures. So $60 billion it is.[180]

A tax figure for that amount does not exist any more than that sales figure itself actually exists. However, we can approximate the taxes based on current taxation in the US. I took the retail sales tax figures from the 50 states and the District of Columbia and averaged them. This yielded a national rate of 4.88%. Applying that rate to the $60 billion annual sales netted $2.9 billion a year in sales tax.[181]

After sales taxes, we move on to excise taxes. This is the infamous "sin tax." We currently charge these excess taxes for both alcohol and cigarettes. To determine the tax rate for alcohol, I took a sample of prices for spirits, wine and beer and applied the national tax rates to each. I then averaged those rates to get to a federal rate of 5.3%. Then I averaged the state excise tax rates and got an additional rate of 3.6%. That results in a total of 8.9% for alcohol. For cigarettes, I averaged the cost of three top brands. I then averaged the various state excise taxes. I compared the taxes to the cost of the smokes and got a rate of 38%.[182]

It's anybody's guess what the actual excise tax rate will be for legalized drugs. However, it would seem to be similar to either the tax on alcohol or cigarettes. Or both. Averaging the two rates gets us to 24%. Using that number, the annual excise tax would be $14.4 billion. While that amount may seem high, a television commentator estimated the total tax take to be nearly $33 billion![183]

There is much less question about the income taxes. The lowest rate is 15%. We'll use that rate to estimate the income taxes that would be garnered by the government. If the retail value of the drugs is $60 billion, the wholesale value is at least half of that. That brings us down to $30 billion. If half of those wholesale prices are related to salaries, we are down to $15 billion. At 15%, the income tax on the field hands and lab rats who will process the drugs would be $2.25 billion.

But it's not just the blue collar boys that have to pony up. Corporations have to pay income tax as well. In this case, where billions of dollars are involved, the rate would be 35%. But that would only be the case if the company's lawyers were lame asses. Billion dollar companies do not retain such lawyers. They hire brutally ambitious, bottom-line conscious lawyers who would [insert your favorite lawyer joke here]. These attorneys would find every available loophole possible. We'll say that they are able to cut the rate in half. That would bring the rate down to 17.5%. I smell bonuses! Applying the new rate to (17.5%) to the sales total ($60 Billion), we get a corporate tax liability of $10.5 billion.[184]

The total tax is listed in the following table:

SALES TAXES	$ 2,900,000,000
EXCISE TAXES	14,400,000,000
INCOME TAXES	2,250,000,000
CORPORATE TAXES	10,500,000,000
TOTAL TAXES	**$30,050,000,000**

These figures were figured out in an admittedly creative manner but, nevertheless, it gives us a rough idea of how much money the Treasury is losing annually.

EXPENDITURES

While we are busy dropping a cool thirty billion, we are also hitting up the Secretary of the Treasury for billions more for enforcement. At the Federal level, we have the Department of Justice, The Department of Homeland Security, The Department of State and the US Armed Services. Some of the efforts of these agencies are concentrated within the borders of the United States. Other programs, eradication for example, are carried out in other countries by the US military. Obviously, this costs a lot of money.

The Department of Justice (DOJ) spends a big ol' pile of that cash. Its budget for Fiscal Year 2008 was over $13.6 billion. The list of the DOJ Agencies that spent those funds is more than two pages long. Some examples are the Drug Enforcement Agency (DEA), The Federal Bureau of Prisons, The Federal Bureau of Investigation (FBI), INTERPOL - US National Central Bureau, The National Drug Intelligence Center and the Office of the Attorney General. All of these have drug related expenses.

We'll look at two of them: The DEA and the Federal Bureau of Prisons.[185]

At the top of the list is the Drug Enforcement Agency. These boys can spend some money too. The 2008 budget for this one department was almost $2.5 billion! That is nearly one-fifth of the total DOJ budget, just to catch druggies and their suppliers. Now, to be fair, ten percent of that money was spent on diversion control, like seizing drugs. That left $2.25 billion for chasing down drug dealers. That chase required the operation of an agency with a staff of 10,774 employees. Those employees were split about 50/50 between agents and support staff. And what did we get for our hard earned money? We got 26,425 arrests. That averages out to a little over $85,000 per arrest. Per <u>arrest</u>, mind you. That does not include prosecution or incarceration. The DEA does not do those things. Those things are extra, like batteries. Of course, like the absent batteries, the arrests are useless without the subsequent prosecution and incarceration. So we will be paying for those later on down the road.[186]

While our focus here is on Federal agencies, it is worthwhile to estimate the cost of the drug wars at the city level. I added the budgets of five large U.S. cities and compared those expenditures with the populations of those cities. I then extrapolated those costs across the nation and reduced the total down to the 20% that we have determined represents the drug costs. The table that follows estimates the annual cost to the cities of the United States at $23 billion.

CITY	POPULATION	POLICE BUDGET
CHICAGO	2,900,000	$1,200,000,000
DALLAS	1,200,000	$455,000,000
LOS ANGELES	4,000,000	$1,000,000,000
NEW YORK	8,300,000	$3,600,000,000
SAN DIEGO	1,400,000	$434,000,000
TOTAL	**17,800,000**	**$6,689,000,000**

Cost per Person	$376
U.S. Population	306,000,000
TOTAL U.S. COST FOR CITIES	$115,056,000,000
COST OF DRUG PREVENTION @ 20%	$23,011,200,000

187

Another place that we have been spending and will continue to spend money is the Federal Bureau of Prisons. The budget for 2008 was $5.3 billion. While the percentage of inmates incarcerated for drug related offences has dropped (from 60% in 1995) to 53%, that is still an annual outlay of $2.8 billion. And the problem gets much worse when we add in the state expenditures.[188]

While our focus is on Federal agencies, it is useful here to take a look at some local numbers. The size of the problem at the Federal level is dwarfed by the total expenditures by the fifty states. In 2008 America had over 2.3 million inmates in her prisons, excluding juveniles. The annual cost of incarcerating those men and women runs more than $20,000 per inmate. Add to that the cost of parole and probation and the total bill for 2008 was $49 billion. Of that total, nearly 20% was related to drug offenses. That is $9.8 billion a year to pop pot heads and jail junkies. It seems a bit steep to me. In fact, it represents an increase of more than 125% over the last 20 years. Notably, during that same time period, spending on education increased only slightly more than 20% The more people we put in prison, the more it costs. [189]

Which brings us to another developing problem - the costs of overcrowding in our prisons. A prime example of this problem is the conditions in the prisons in California. Over 150,000 inmates in that state are crammed like sardines into facilities meant to house a little more than half of that. In December of 2008, a panel determined that the treatment of prisoners in that state constituted cruel and unusual punishment. That constitution was therefore found to be unconstitutional and in February, 2009, judges in Federal court ruled that the state would have to release thousands of prisoners, up to one third of the inmates currently held. [190]

A Federal receiver, J. Clark Kelso, was appointed to oversee the correction of the overcrowded conditions. Kelso asked for $8 billion dollars from the state of California to accomplish that task. The state, already in deep financial trouble, was not forthcoming with the funds. State officials claimed that the steps that they had already taken, spending $2 billion on inmate health and shipping nearly 20,000 prisoners to other states and other outside facilities, has put the state in a position to handle the situation itself. [191]

I believe that the state would be better able to handle the situation by simply releasing the 20% of its inmates that are incarcerated for drug offenses. That would be 30,000 of the 150,000 inmates that are currently held.

A release of thirty thousand men and women would go a long way toward easing the overcrowding of those facilities.

Overcrowded or not, the cost of prisons in America is prohibitive. In 2007, the Feds spent $5 billion on prisons. Fifty-three per cent of that money is spent on druggies. That's about $2.65 billion. The states spent $49 billion. At twenty per cent, that's $9.8 billion up in smoke. The grand total is $12.45 billion out of the pockets of American taxpayers.[192]

And now back to the Feds. Leaving the prison system, we move on to the Department of Homeland Security. This is a relatively new agency, proposed by President Bush as a reaction to the terrorist attacks on New York City on September 11, 2001. The official beginning of the Cabinet level Department was on March 1, 2003. The Department, which within five years of its inception had grown to a bureaucracy with a budget of almost $38 billion, contains three agencies that are of interest to us. They are the US Customs and Border Protection, The US Coast Guard and Counter-Narcotics Enforcement. US Customs and Border Protection is an obvious choice for deeper discussion. Possibly less so is the US Coast Guard, which has a surprisingly large role in the rounding up of cocaine cowboys and other drug dealers.[193]

First up is U.S. Customs and Border Protection (CBP), with a 2008 budget of $8.8 billion. These guys have been around for a long time. The very first United States Congress created this agency with only the fifth piece of legislation ever passed in this country. Its purpose was to collect cash from import tariffs and to regulate those imports. It has historically done a bang up job collecting money, currently some $90 million a day, but the regulation part has been a little tougher road to hoe.[194]

Regulation is trickier because the bad guys don't fill out forms and submit payments like the good guys do. So the Customs officers have to catch the bad guys and put them in jail. In that capacity, they employ nearly 20,000 officers to make over 70 arrests and confiscate over 7,500 pounds of narcotics a day. That's a little over 25,500 arrests annually for the 20,000 cops! Just over one apiece. Not terribly efficient. Curiously, they also seize 435 "pests" daily. Note to my ex-wives, you might want to steer clear of the Mexican border. I'm just sayin'.[195]

Of course, CBP also seizes 2.7 million pounds of drugs annually, patrols nearly 7,000 miles of border and employs some of its employees for collecting tariffs, not drugs. So to be fair, we'll cut the staff in half. That's brings our arrest record per officer to a whoppin' 2 apiece! For only $8.8 billion. Whoops, fair is fair, better cut the budget in half too. So now it's only $4.4 billion dollars for the 25,500 arrests. Wow, I feel much better now.[196]

Also helping to take drugs and their dealers off the streets, although technically here it's the ocean, is the other drug enforcement agency that we are going to visit: The US Coast Guard. One of the functions of the Coast Guard is drug interdiction, using ships and aircraft. In this capacity, the Coast Guard seizes illegal drug shipments and makes associated arrests. In fact, the Coast Guard is responsible for over 50% of all the annual US cocaine seizures. In 2008, the Guard seized or removed more than 367,000 pounds of the powder. They also picked up over 22,000 pounds of pot. In addition, the Guard arrested (only) 196 people. And the cost of those activities? Just over ten percent of the Coast Guard's budget in 2008. That would be a total anti-drug expenditure of just under $1 billion a year.[197]

UNINTENDED
CONSEQUENCES

In 2010, Arizona passed Senate bill 1070, which addressed illegal immigration into that state. Arizona had become a valley through which drug dealers and human smugglers snuck their illegal products into the rest of the United States. The law was written in response to the exponential rise in crime that those immigrant criminals inflicted on the people of Arizona. In order to see how that law negatively affects Arizona and the rest of the nation, first we must examine the law itself.

The law allowed that "for any lawful contact by a law enforcement official ... where reasonable suspicion exists that the person is an alien ... a reasonable attempt shall be made ... to determine the immigration status of the person." It goes on to state that "a law enforcement officer, without a warrant, may arrest a person if the officer has probable cause to believe that the person has committed any public offense that makes the person removable from the United States [e.g. illegal immigration]."[198]

Detractors of this law called it racist. Supporters of the law insisted that it was not racist. They claimed that the law was aimed at criminals and their actions, not at a particular race. They were, perhaps, referring to scenes like the one in Pinal County in June, 2010, in which two Latino men, assumed to be smugglers of people or pot, were killed by AK-47 wielding attackers, also presumed to be Mexican smugglers. This attack took place in a part of Arizona in which drug smuggling from across the Mexican border is common. More that a million pounds of pot were confiscated by drug enforcement officials in Arizona in 2009.[199]

Supporters might also point to the almost daily reports of kidnappings in Arizona. Those kidnappings were often payback for drug related beefs - failure to pay for drugs for instance. Ransoms of up to $1,000,000 have been reported. The victims of those kidnappings have been viciously tortured and sometimes killed. Other kidnappings were simply motivated by money. Some Arizonans have been kidnapped and held just long enough to run their ATM cards to their limit.[200]

The law is blatantly racist (the cops will be making "lawful contact" with Latinos suspected of smuggling drugs and humans, not Nigerians suspected of smuggling ivory or Belgians bypassing Customs with cartons of chocolate). But that is not the issue that we are interested in here. We want to look at the negative effect that the law is having on both Arizona and the other 49 states.

There have been reactions from both sides of this issue. Right wing supporters organized a demonstration in Arizona in June, 2010. That was not the only pro-SB1070 demonstration to be held in Arizona. A Californian candidate, running for the governor's office, made a point of agreeing with the law. One poll counted 60 per cent of Americans in favor of the law. On the other side of the issue, demonstrations have been held all over the country against the law, Many organizations have stated their opposition to the law, including the AFL-CIO and the Major League Baseball Players Association. Cities across the nation, from Los Angeles, California to St. Paul, Minnesota to Hartford, Connecticut, have called for economic boycotts against the state of Arizona. Almost twenty conventions have cancelled their plans to meet in Arizona. Tourists are cancelling as well. Even president Obama has come out against it.[201]

So the law has ignited a kind of civil war. Americans are pitted against other Americans on this issue. Brothers against brothers. Tempers are flaring and politicians are ranting. Arizona is seeing other cities attempting to cancel contracts. Conventions and tourism are taking a huge hit. And all because of the ongoing sale of illegal drugs by criminals.

And while we're talking about laws, let's look at some peripheral drug laws. Every state in the union has laws governing the behavior of drug users. Those laws should be amended to read exactly the same as the laws for alcohol users. As examples, we'll look at three laws in particular: the legal age for consumption of drugs, driving while high on drugs and committing crimes, such as shoplifting or burglary.

Just as with the laws governing consumption of alcohol, minors should not be allowed to use drugs. Some would argue that the best age for legal consumption would be twenty-one. While that age limit is workable, I believe that eighteen is old enough. At eighteen, citizens of the United States are adults. They can vote and they can join the armed services to fight for our country. I believe that they should also be able to smoke a joint while watching a movie at home with their honey.

However, driving high is another thing altogether. Driving a motor vehicle while intoxicated on any substance, drugs or alcohol, is dangerous to both the driver and to everyone on the road nearby that driver. Anyone caught driving under the influence of drugs should be given the same criminal penalties as they would receive if they were driving drunk on alcohol.

Likewise, laws against shoplifting, burglary, etc., should not change simply because consumption of a particular drug had been legalized. If a drug user has stolen something or robbed someone, he should be prosecuted for those crimes, regardless of their motivation.

And while most folks aren't motivated to commit crimes, some will be motivated, simply due to legalization, to smoke some reefer. And that worries a lot of other people. These worried citizens fear that legalizing drugs will turn America into a pill popping, pot smoking nation of junkies. They fear that the most powerful and prosperous country in the history of mankind will be reduced to a giant opium den, ripe for a takeover by our adversaries.

I beg to differ. The country outlawed alcohol early in the Twentieth century. After that dismal failure, they reopened the bars and stocked the liquor stores with 80 proof party drinks. The country did not become a nation of alcoholics. Eighty years later, liquor is still legal and we are still not addicted to the stuff. We do have our share of people who have a problem with alcohol but they are the exception, not the rule.

This is exactly what will happen with legalized drugs. Some folks will take the drugs but most will not. Some people will become junkies but the rest of us know that that road is a dead end. Literally.

Eighty years hence, the citizens of our great country will shake their heads at our short sighted drug policy just as we, today, see the folly of the alcohol prohibition.

FREE USE OF "SOFT" DRUGS

As we have seen, the United States government has spent, and is spending, billions of dollars and putting thousands of people in prison because it thinks that life with legal drugs would be a catastrophe. We are going to look at two places where pot is semi-legal. Those two utopian havens of high are the legendary Amsterdam, in The Netherlands and our own left coast depository of all things "out there" - Los Angeles, California.

We have all heard the stories of party town, earth - Amsterdam. Drugs are legal and the party is on! Wrong, wrong, wrong. Drugs are illegal in Amsterdam. "But, but ..." , you stammer! Just sit down and listen.

Hard drugs are illegal. Soft drugs are only illegal on paper. The manufacture, distribution, sale and use of cocaine, heroin and all the other hard drugs will get you put in jail. Technically, that is true of the soft drugs, pot and hash, as well. However, the Opium Act of 1976 effectively decriminalized the soft drugs. So, my little drug tourist, with the personal use of 5 grams or less of pot or hash, the officer who busts you can simply drop the charges. - a kind of "catch and release" program. Barring any other extenuating circumstances, that is what the policeman would do. However, you would not even be bothered by the police if you were in the preferred place to consume cannabis, the famous "coffee shops."[202]

Ah, the coffee shops. Here, one can buy some pot "for here or to go," just like you favorite fast food place. Except that they do not have drive-thru service. They do have rules, however. You must be eighteen or older. You may only buy 5 grams at a time. You may not get rowdy in the coffee shops. In order to keep the order, alcohol cannot be sold in the coffee houses. Alcohol makes people do stupid things. But the best rule of all concerns tobacco. Tobacco has historically been added to the pot in order to cut down the potency. This is a good thing. Amsterdam grass is a lot stronger than the dirt weed y'all have been smoking. You can select different mixes of grass and tobacco to fit your personal preferences. The two most important features are how strong the weed is and how raspy it is on your throat. But there's a problem. In 2008, a new law was passed. While smoking pot indoors remains semi-legal, smoking tobacco indoors is against the law. Come on, now that's funny! I can see the cop now. "Son, you got any tobacco mixed in with them drugs? Hell, I'll run yer ass in right now!" Some shops now actually have a *tobacco* smoking area where you can legally smoke "tobacco laced" pot! Honestly, you just can't make this stuff up![203]

So, now that Amsterdam's citizens are free from second hand smoke, let's see how the liberalized drug laws are helping to keep consumers safe. A study in 2001 compared some two and a half decades of Dutch legal weed to the same time period in "lock-em-up" America.

The study found that pot use in The Netherlands was half that of Americans. Part of that reduction was from the loss of the glamour factor associated with legal weed. The same study showed that the Netherlands had a lower rate of heroin use and a lower overall average expenditure on drugs.[204]

The lesson in Amsterdam is that legal marijuana is not a problem for society. In fact, it exhibits the benefits that we have extolled throughout this book. The coffee houses make money and they pay taxes. They do not allow roughhousing. People smoking cannabis for pleasure do not go to jail. They just go home. And, overall drug use is lower, in part because the "cool factor" is gone.

Another place where pot is cool is in California. In 1996, the people of that state, crazy as they are, passed a law allowing the use of medical marijuana. That law, ballot Proposition 215, says that patients, their helpers and their doctors are not subject to prosecution by the state of California, simply for possession or use of the drug. Federal laws are not affected, of course, and initially, some medical marijuana suppliers were raided by the Feds. President Obama has said that his administration would not conduct those type of raids.[205]

It would take a lot of raids. The LA City Council listed 800 shops when they passed restrictions on local dispensaries in April, 2010. A simple internet search brought up nearly 300 of those dispensaries. Perusing the list, I spotted a shop only two blocks from my house. There were two more a few blocks further, one about a mile north, fifteen in the mid-valley.[206]

These dispensaries have rules. The fees for opening one of those dispensaries total nearly $1,600. No alcohol can be sold there. A separate smoking area must be provided. Sound familiar?[207]

And how have these shops of sin affected California's communities? Crime went down. Really. Between 1996, when the proposition was passed, and 2008, assaults in California dropped from 500 per 100,000 of population to about 290. Robberies dropped from about 400 to 150. Property crimes sank from about 2,400 to some 1,750. Put that in your pipe and smoke it.[208]

FOR EXAMPLE

I present here two fictitious scenarios in which an ounce of marijuana is provided for consumption at a party in Los Angeles. One scenario takes place in the present drug war culture and the second one takes place after legalization. We begin during the drug war:

The marijuana is grown and in a foreign country by foreign workers. Guys with guns buy the pot from the growers for next to nothing. No taxes are paid. These gangsters, when they aren't shooting each other over territorial rights, smuggle the weed into the United States. Every day, the United States pays thousands of various law enforcement agents to stop these killers from importing their pot. The cops usually fail to do that. That is the case here too and so the weed makes it across the border intact. No Customs duties are paid. The smuggled weed is sold here in the states to violent street gangs. The local gangs cut the weed with some non-cannabis concoction and spray it with PCP in order to make a bigger profit. They sell their adulterated weed to a buyer on the street. The gang pays no income tax and the buyer pays no sales tax.

The buyer takes the pot to his party. Two young users end up in the emergency room, sickened by the unregulated weed.

Scenario two takes place after legalization. The marijuana is grown on a farm here in the States. The farm has twenty employees, none of whom own a gun and all of whom pay income taxes. The farmer reports all of his sales and pays his taxes promptly on April 15th. The raw Marijuana is transported by an American trucking firm to a factory where it is converted to pre-packaged pot. The pot is subject to FDA regulations and is monitored for purity by FDA regulators. The lab packages the pot for retail sale in neat one ounce packs. The lab reports all of its sales and pays its taxes on time. The laboratory owner owns neither a machine gun nor a machete. The lab ships the pot to liquor stores for resale to retail customers, using the very same American trucking firm that the grower had used. The liquor store sells the goods to our party guy. Our party guy pays for the pot, including the excessive sin tax, and takes it back to the party. No one gets sick. No one gets shot.

AND SO ...

I started this book by laying out the main premise - that the various costs of America's failed war on drugs were simply too high for the country to absorb.

Those costs included the various aspects of criminal behavior committed to sustain drug sales: smuggling, organized crime, terrorism, gangs, adulteration of the product, killings and kidnappings. Those costs also include the actual financial costs of the war on drugs: loss of sales tax revenue, loss of income tax revenues, the cost of law enforcement and the cost of the prison system. Taken as a whole, the staggering cost of the war on drugs is evidence of a war that we are losing, day by day. Let's review.

Drug smuggling has taken place in many locations and by many methods. But in both Prohibition and the war on drugs, the northern and southern borders have been particularly porous. Of the two borders, smuggling along Mexico's borders has been the most dangerous to the American people. Legalization would stop that traffic on a dime.

Dollars, not dimes, have funded the various criminal organizations in America and all over the world. Prohibition brought us the Mafia but the war on drugs has brought us murdering Drug cartels, terrorists and American street gangs. In Mexico, the country has leaned toward anarchy as the Cartels murder anyone in their tracks. And that includes innocent Americans, killed or kidnapped in Mexico and right here in the United States. Worldwide, terrorists have killed our young servicemen and women and threatened our very way of life. Here at home, street gangs have gunned down innocent people. All of those organizations sell drugs to keep themselves in power. If we take away the drug money, we cut out the heart of these killers.

And they are killing us without guns as well. As there is no government inspection of the drugs to ensure a safe product for the consumer, dealers often take shortcuts. To increase their profit, they cut their drugs with various, often dangerous, substances. During Prohibition, they added wood alcohol to the whisky. This killed some people but boosted the bottom line. The drugsters do the same thing. They have added all sorts of nefarious products to the pot, coke and junk that they sell. Predictably, consumers have been killed by the inconsistent potency of the drugs that they consume. If the drugs were legal, they would be subject to FDA rules. The product's potency would be the same from batch to batch and the American consumer would be safer.

And the taxpayers would be richer. The financial costs associated with the war on drugs has been astronomical. The Federal government has lost, and is continuing to lose, all of the sales taxes, income taxes and corporate taxes that should have been generated by the legal sales of drugs. By our count, that is somewhere in the range of $30 billion a year. Of course, we also have to add the outpouring of cash for law enforcement and incarceration to those lost revenues. We pegged that number at about $23 billion annually. By our calculation, which is most probably on the low side, we can save in excess of $50 billion dollars a year by legalizing all drugs.

Interestingly, we have seen that in the places where drugs (well, to be fair, marijuana) have been legalized, crime has not increased, as some would want you to believe.

So, just as with alcohol Prohibition, the war on drugs has been a painful, costly mistake. The human and financial costs associated with the suppression of drugs are just too high. With Prohibition, the American public learned that lesson in a little over a decade. We have not learned that lesson, however, in a *century* of fighting drugs.

We need to erase all of the anti-drug laws currently on the books. The Cartels, terrorists and street gangs will not be able to exist, certainly not at any where near the level at which they now exist, without the benefit of the cash inflow that the sale of drugs brings them. Legalization will create jobs in the growth and manufacture of drugs for recreational consumption. We will be able to regulate the drugs and tax the drugs. Heavily. The only rational answer to America's foolish war on drugs is:

LEGALIZE 'EM!

BIBLIOGRAPHY

Bergreen, Laurence. Capone The Man and the Era. New York: Touchstone, 1994.

Capeci, Jerry. The Complete Idiot's Guide to The Mafia. Indianapolis: Alpha Books, 2002.

Donziger, Steven R. The Real War on Crime. New York: Harper Collins, 1996

Lieurance, Suzanne. The Prohibition Era. Berkeley Heights, NJ: Enslow Publishers, 2003.

Miron, Jeffrey A. Drug War Crimes. Oakland: The Independent Institute, 2004.

Nelli, Hubert S. The Business of Crime. Chicago: Oxford University Press, 1976.

WEBWORK

PROHIBITION

(Endnotes)

1   "History of alcohol Prohibition." <http://
     ww.druglibrary.org/schaffer/LIBRARY/studies/nc/
     nc2a.htm>"Prohibition Laws." <http://www.library.
     thinkquest.org/04oct/00492/prohibition_laws.
     htm>

2   "History of alcohol Prohibition." <http://
     ww.druglibrary.org/schaffer/LIBRARY/studies/nc/
     nc2a.htm>

3   "History of alcohol Prohibition." <http://
     ww.druglibrary.org/schaffer/LIBRARY/studies/nc/
     nc2a.htm>nc2a.htm

4   "Carry Amelia Nation." Kansas State Historical
     Society.   <http://www.kshs.org/people/Nation_
     Carry.html>

5   "History of alcohol Prohibition." <http://
     ww.druglibrary.org/schaffer/LIBRARY/studies/nc/
     nc2a.htm>

6   "Volstead Act." HistoryCentral.com. <http://www.
     multied.com/documents/Volstead.act.html>

7   Mason, Phillip P. "Anyone Who Couldn't Get a
     Drink Wasn't Tryin'." MichiganHistoryOnline
     <http://www.michiganhistorymagazine.com/
     extra/2008/marapr/couldnt_get_drink.html

8   Ibid   "Prohibition: No Liquor Allowed." Suite 101.
     com <http://www. CanadianHistory.suite101.com/
     article.cfm/prohibition_no_longer_allowed>

9   Mason, Phillip P. "Anyone Who Couldn't Get a
     Drink Wasn't Tryin'." MichiganHistoryOnline

10   Mason, Phillip P. "Anyone Who Couldn't Get a
     Drink Wasn't Tryin'." MichiganHistoryOnline

11   Ibid

12   McWilliams, Peter. "Ain't Nobody's Business if
     You Do." <http://www.McWilliams.com/books/
     aint/402.htm>

13   The New York Times Archives. "Ex-Revenue Men
     Accused."   <http://www.query.nytimes.com/gst/
     abstract.html>

14   McWilliams, Peter. "Ain't Nobody's Business if
     You Do." <http://www.McWilliams.com/books/
     aint/402.htm>

15   "Organized Crime." <http://www.deathreference.
     com/nu-pu/organized-crime.html>   Capeci,
     Jerry. The Complete Idiot's Guide to the Mafia.
     Indianapolis:Alpha Books, 2002.

16   Buchanan, Edna. "Lucky Luciano." <http://time.
     com/time/time100/builder/profile/Luciano.html>

17   Buchanan, Edna. "Lucky Luciano." <http://time.com/time/time100/builder/profile/Luciano.html>

18   Ibid

19   Ibid. Nelli, Humbert. The Business of Crime. Chicago:The Oxford University Press. 1976. Pg 207.

20   Bergreen, Laurence. Capone, The Man and the Era. New York:Touchstone, 1994

21   Bergreen, Laurence. Capone, The Man and the Era. New York:Touchstone, 1994

22   Ibid

23   Ibid

24   Ibid

25   Ibid

26   Capeci, Jerry. The Complete Idiot's Guide to the Mafia. Indianapolis:Alpha Books, 2002. Lieurance, Suzanne. The Prohibition Era In American History. Enslow Publishers,2003   Thorton, Mark."Alcohol Prohibition was a Failure." Cato Institute. <http://www.cato.org/pubs/psd/pa-157.html>

27   "Fiorella LaGuardia on Prohibition." Ohio State University, College of Humanities. <http://www.prohibition.osu.edu/content/Laguardi.com>

28   Lieurance, Suzanne. The Prohibition Era In American History. Enslow Publishers,2003. Capeci, Jerry. The Complete Idiot's Guide to the Mafia. Indianapolis:Alpha Books, 2002.

29   <http://www.stlouisfed.org/publications/income/page/12526/download/33660/12526_1915-1930.

pdf>" Wickersham Commission Report <http://www.druglibrary.org/schaffer/library/studies/wick/index.html> Mason, Phillip P. "Anyone Who Couldn't Get a Drink Wasn't Tryin'." MichiganHistoryOnline

30 McWilliams, Peter "Ain't Nobody's Business If You Do"< http://www.McWilliams.com/books/aint/402.htm> Thorton, Mark. "Alcohol Prohibition Was a Failure." <http://www.cato.org/pubs/pas/pa-157.html>

31 McWilliams, Peter "Ain't Nobody's Business If You Do" <http://www.McWilliams.com/books/aint/402.htm>

32 "Pure Food and Drug Act." <http://coursea.matrix.msu.edu/~hst203/documents/pure.html

33 Ibid Thorton, Mark. "Alcohol Prohibition Was a Failure." <http://www.cato.org/pubs/pas/pa-157.html>

34 Capeci, Jerry. The Complete Idiot's Guide to the Mafia. Indianapolis:Alpha Books, 2002.

35 Thorton, Mark. "Alcohol Prohibition Was a Failure." <http://www.cato.org/pubs/pas/pa-157.html>

36 McWilliams, Peter "Ain't Nobody's Business If You Do" <http://www.McWilliams.com/books/aint/402.htm>

37 Ibid

38 Ibid

39 Lieurance, Suzanne. The Prohibition Era In American History. Enslow Publishers,2003 <http://

www.prohibition.osu.edu/content/laguardi.cfm>
<http://www.taxanalysts.com.>

40   Wickersham Commission Report< http://www.
     druglibrary.org/schaffer/library/studies/wick/index.
     html Thorton, Mark. "Alcohol Prohibition Was a
     Failure."   <http://www.cato.org/pubs/pas/pa-157.
     html

41   Ibid

42   Wickersham Commission Report< http://www.
     druglibrary.org/schaffer/library/studies/wick/
     index.html>   McWilliams, Peter "Ain't Nobody's
     Business If You Do" <http://www.McWilliams.com/
     books/aint/402.htm>   Thorton, Mark. "Alcohol
     Prohibition Was a Failure." <http://www.cato.org/
     pubs/pas/pa-157.html>

43   Ibid

44   Ibid   Lieurance, Suzanne. The Prohibition Era In
     American History. Enslow Publishers,2003.

45   McWilliams, Peter "Ain't Nobody's Business If
     You Do" <http://www.McWilliams.com/books/
     aint/402.htm>

46   Ibid

47   Thorton, Mark. "Alcohol Prohibition Was a
     Failure."   <http://www.cato.org/pubs/pas/pa-157.
     html> Capeci, Jerry. The Complete Idiot's Guide
     to the Mafia. Indianapolis:Alpha Books, 2002.

48   Thorton, Mark. "Alcohol Prohibition Was a
     Failure."   <http://www.cato.org/pubs/pas/pa-157.
     html><http:www.amhist.unomaha.edu/module_
     files/statistics%20ON%20prohibition.rtf>

DRUGS

49 "Marijuana History." <http://www.students.missouri.edu/~norml/facts.htm>

50 Ibid "Medical Marijuana: A History." <http://www.time.com/time/covers/1101021/hixtory.html>

51 Herer, Jack. "The Emperor wears no clothes" http://jackherer.com/chapter12.html "Drug Use: A U.S. Concern for Over a Century." <http://usinfo.state.gov/journals/itgic/0697/ijge/gi-8.htm>

52 Herer, Jack. "The Emperor wears no clothes" <http://jackherer.com/chapter12.html> Herer, Jack. "The Emperor wears no clothes" <http://jackherer.com/chapter13.html >

53 "Medical Marijuana: A History." http://www.time.com/time/covers/1101021/hixtory.html> "History of Marihuana Use: Medical and Intoxicant." <http://www.druglibrary.org/schaffer/Library/studies/nc/ncla_3.htm>

54 Ibid Herer, Jack. "The Emperor wears no clothes" <http://jackherer.com/chapter12.html>

55 "The Racial History of US Drug Possession."<http//www.drugp;olicy.org/about/position/race_paper_history.cfm>"History of Marijuana Legislation." http://www.druglibrary.org/schaffer/library/studies/nc/nc2_7.htm >

56 "Opium Throughout History", <http://www.pbs.org/wgbh/pages/frontline/shows/heroin/etc/history.html>

57 Ibid

58   Ibid

59   Ibid

60   Ibid

61   "European Mercantilism (1773-1858)." <http://www.a1b2c3.com/drugs/opi009.htm>

62   Ibid

63   Ibid

64   Allingham, Phillip V. "England and China: The Opium Wars, 1839-60." <http://www.victorianweb.org/history/empire/opiumwars/opiumwars1.html>

65   Ibid

66   Ibid   "European Mercantilism (1773-1858)." <http://www.a1b2c3.com/drugs/opi009.htm>

67   Ibid

68   "The Racial History of US Drug Possession."<http//www.drugp;olicy.org/about/position/race_paper_history.cfm>   "Opium Throughout History", <http://www.pbs.org/wgbh/pages/frontline/shows/heroin/etc/history.html>

69   Ibid

70   Ibid

71   "History of Cocaine – The 'Miracle Drug'" <http://www.roadjunky.com/guide/829/history-of-cocaine-the-miracle-drug>

72   Ibid

73   Ibid

74   Ibid

75   "History of Cocaine and crack use." <http://www. intheknowzone.com/cocaine/history.htm>

76   Ibid   "The History of Cocaine." <http:// michaelshouse.com/cocaine-addiction/history-of-cocaine.html>

77   "Cocaine." <http://www.intheknowzone.com/cocaine/history.htm>

78   Time U.S. "Freud's Cocaine Capers." <http://www. time.com/time/magazine/article/0,9171,912660. html?promoid+googlep

79   Ibid

80   Frontline. "The Columbian Cartels" <http:// www.pbs.org/wgbh/pages/frontline/shows/drugs/ business/inside/columbian.html>

81   "The Racial History of US Drug Possession."<http// www.drugp;olicy.org/about/position/race_paper_ history.cfm>

82   "Federal Legislation of the 20th Century." <http:// www.usml.edu/~keelr/180/law.html>

83   "Pure Food and Drug Act." <http://coursea.matrix. msu.edu/~hst203/documents/pure.html>

84   Ibid

85   "The Consumers Union Report on Licit and Illicit Drugs." <http://www.druglibrary.org/schaffer/ Library/studies/cu/cu8.html>

86   Ibid

87   Ibid

88   Ibid

89   "The Marihuana Act of 1937." <http://www. druglibrary.org/schaffer/hemp/taxact/mjtaxact. htm>

90   Ibid

91   "Additional Statement of H.J. Anslinger, Commissioner of Narcotics." <http://hempfarm. org/Papers/Hearing_Transcript_2html>

92   "The Report of the National Commission on Marihuana and Drug Abuse." <http://www. drugLibrary.org/schaffer/Library/studies/nc/nc2_7. htm>

93   History of Marijuana Legislation." http://www. druglibrary.org/schaffer/library/studies/nc/nc2_7. htm >

94   "History of Marijuana Legislation." http://www. druglibrary.org/schaffer/library/studies/nc/nc2_7. htm >"Federal Legislation of the 20th Century." <http://www.usml.edu/~keelr/180/law.html>

95   Ibid

96   Fields, Gary and Scheck, Justin "U.S. Mellows on Medical Marijuana" 20 Oct 2009<http://www.mpp. org/states/federal/us-mellows-on-medical.html>

97   "Drug Trafficking Organizations." <http://www. usdoj.gov/dea/concern/18862/dtos.htm>

98   "United Nations Activities." 2001. <http://www. ncjrs.gov/pdffiles1/nij/218561.pdf>

99   Ibid

100   Ibid

101　"Drug Trafficking Organizations." <http://www. usdoj.gov/dea/concern/18862/dtos.htm>

102　"US Customs today." 2000. <http://www.customs. gov/custoday/jul2000/conceal.htm>

103　"Drug Smuggling." <http://www.criminal-law-lawyer-source.com/terms/smuggling.html>

104　"CRS Report for Congress." 2007.<http://www.fas. org/sgp/crs/row/RL34215.pdf>

105　"Pablo Escobar." <http://www.medellintraveler. com/escobar.html>

106　Ibid

107　Ibid "Drugs & Terror: Just the Facts." <http://www. drugstory.org/pdfs/drugsterror_factsheet.pdf>

108　"Pablo Escobar." <http://www.medellintraveler. com/escobar.html>

109　"The Columbian Cartels." http://www.pbs.org/ wgbh/pages/frontline/shows/drugs/business/inside/ columbian.html   "Cali drug chiefs given 30-year prison terms." 2008<http://www.udstoday.com/ news/nation/2006-09-26-columbian-kingpins_x. htm>

110　The Columbian Cartels." http://www.pbs.org/ wgbh/pages/frontline/shows/drugs/business/inside/ columbian.html

111　Ibid

112　"The Columbian Cartels." http://www.pbs.org/ wgbh/pages/frontline/shows/drugs/business/inside/ columbian.html

113 "CRS Report for Congress." 2007.<http://www.fas.org/sgp/crs/row/RL34215.pdf>

114 Ibid   <http://www.pbs.org/wgbh/pages/frontline/shows/drugs/business/place.html>

115 "CRS Report for Congress." 2007.<http://www.fas.org/sgp/crs/row/RL34215.pdf>   <http://www.reuters.com/article/latest/Crisis/idUSN18483088>

116 Ibid

117 "GRENADE ATTACK." Daily News [LA] 17Sept.2008:A8., "7 DEAD IN ATTACKS." Daily News 11Nov.2008:A7., "7 BODIES DUMPED." Daily News [LA] 26Nov.2008:A8.

118 <http://www.pbs.org/wgbh/pages/frontline/shows/drugs/business/place.html>

119 Ibid

120 Ibid. "CRS Report for Congress." 2007.<http://www.fas.org/sgp/crs/row/RL34215.pdf>

121 "Drug Cartels" 1997 <http://www.pbs.org/wgbh/pages/frontline/shows/mexico/etc/arellano.html>

122 "BODIES FOUND."   Daily News[LA] 05October2008:A9. "BLOW,BLOOD & THE BORDER." Daily News 27Aug 2008:Sunday Viewpoint. "Death during recess." Los Angeles Times 25Oct2008:Front Page

123 "SIX GUNNED DOWN AT BAR IN MAZATLAN." Daily News 7FEB2010; "RESIDENTS TOLD TO LEAVE - OR ELSE." Daily News 17APR2010.

124 "Drug Cartels." 1997 http://www.pbs.org/wgbh/
pages/frontline/shows/mexico/etc/arellano.html,
"US gives Mexico anti-drug funding." 2008 http://
newsvote.bbc.co.uk/mpapps/pagetools/print/news.
bbc.co.uk/1/hi/world/americas/776..., "SLAYINGS
ESCALATE" Daily News [LA] 9Dec2008:A7

125 "SHOOTING IN STATE OFFICE." Daily News
18Dec2008:A8. "SENIOR OFFICER KILLED."
Daily News 19Dec2008:A8. "NINE MORE
DECAPITATED." Daily News 22Dec2008:A7.
"NO HINT BEFORE CRASH." Daily News
06Nov2008:A8.

126 ibid: "CARTELS TARGET MEXICAN
ARMY IN BRAZEN ATTACKS." Daily News
2Apr2010:A11.

127 http://newsvote.bbc.co.uk/mpapps/pagetools/print/
news.bbc.co.uk/1/hi/world/americas/776"Official
linked to drug trafficking." Daily News
02Aug2008:A6. "Former top cop nabbed in drug
probe." Daily News. 08November2008:A15.
"OFFICIAL ACCUSED." Daily News
22Nov2008:A7. "INTERPOL TO PROBE
LEAKS." Daily News 20Nov2008.

128 "CRS Report for Congress." 2007 <http://www.cas.
org/sgp/crs/row/RL34215.pdf>

129 "US gives Mexico anti-drug funding." 2008.

130 "Gunmen take U.S. biologists by surprise."
Daily News 11Oct2008:A7. "Suspected Hit man
for Mexican cartel held in Texas." Daily News
26Oct2008: A29. "Incomplete tunnel found near
border." Daily News 11Dec2008 :S4."SHERIFF

ARRESTED." Daily News 15Oct2008: A8. "Drug gangs taking over public land." Daily News 02MAR2010:A5.

131 "U.S. consulate worker, spouse killed in Juarez." Daily News 15MAR2010: A9. "Drug war takes growing toll." Daily News 21MAR2010: A16.

132 "Opium poppy harvest declines 6% in Afghanistan." 2008. http://www.latimes.com/news/nationsworld/la-fg-opium29-2008nov28,0,4532484.story, "Al-Qaeda's Drug Trade Keeps Them Afloat During the Economic Crisis." 2008 http://www.huffingtonpost.com/2008/10/16/al-qaedas-drug-trade-keep_n_135352.html?v... "U.S. to target Taliban drug traffic." 2008 <http://usatoday.printthis.clickability.com/pt/cpt?action=U.S.+to+target+Taliban...>

133 "Taliban taking control of valley." 2008 Daily News 30Dec2008: A12

134 "Al-Qaeda's Drug Trade Keeps Them Afloat During the Economic Crisis." 2008 http://www.huffingtonpost.com/2008/10/16/al-qaedas-drug-trade-keep_n_135352.html?v..., "CRS Report for Congress." 2001 <http://www.fpc.state.gov/documents/organization/6210.pdf>

135 "Narco-Terrorism: International Drug Trafficking and Terrorism – A Dangerous Mix." 2003 <http://www.state.gov/p/inl/rls/rm/21129.htm>

136 "FARC,ELN:Colombia'a Left-wing Guerrillas." 2008 http://www.cfr.org/publication/9272/, "Columbia hostage Betancourt freed." 2008 <http://

newsvote.bbc.co.uk/mpaps/pagetools/print/news. bbc.co.uk/2/hi/americas/7486552>

137 "FARC,ELN:Colombia'a Left-wing Guerrillas." 2008 http://www.cfr.org/publication/9272/, "Narco-Terrorism: International Drug Trafficking and Terrorism – A Dangerous Mix." 2003 <http://www.state.gov/p/inl/rls/rm/21129.htm>

138 Ibid "U.S. DRUG RINGS PROBED FOR TIES TO MIDEAST TERRORISTS." 2002. Los Angeles Times 24Dec2002 :A11.

139 "ShiningPath,Tupac Amaru (Peru, leftists)" 2008. <http://www.cfr.org/publication/9276/shining_ path_tupac_amaru_peru_leftists.html>

140 "U.S. DRUG RINGS PROBED FOR TIES TO MIDEAST TERRORISTS." 2002. Los Angeles Times 24Dec2002 :A11. "Narco-Terrorism: International Drug Trafficking and Terrorism – A Dangerous Mix." 2003 <http:/www.state.gov/p/inl/ rls/rm/21129.htm>

141 "Los Angeles-based Gangs – Bloods and Crips." <http://www.dc.state.fl.us/pub/gangs/la.html>

142 "FEDERAL RACKETEERING CHARGES FILED AGAINST CRIPS GANG MEMBERS IN WICHITA." 2007 <http://www.usdoj.gov/usao/ks/ press/Sept07/09_29a.html>

143 "Los Angeles-based Gangs – Bloods and Crips." http://www.dc.state.fl.us/pub/gangs/la.html "'Playboy Blood' Gang Members Charged with Racketeering, Murder, and Drug Trafficking." 2008 <http://www.backgroundnow.com/blog/

background-check/playboy-blod-gang-members-charged-with-racketeering-muder-and-drug-trafficking-offenses/>

144 Ibid

145 Ibid

146 "MS-13 gang growing extremely dangerous, FBI says" 2005 <http://usatoday.com/news/nation/2006-01-05-gang-grows_x.htm >

147 Ibid

148 Ibid

149 Ibid

150 Ibid

151 Daily News [LA] 09Sep2004: 11

152 Daily News [LA] 07Feb2007 :5

153 "18 members of MacArthur Park area gang are indicted." 2007. <http://www.streetgangs.com/topics/2007/102507eight.html>

154 "MOTORCYCLE GANG VIOLENCE: Laughlin event turns deadly." 2002 http://www.reviewjournal.com "LAUGHLIN MELEE: Biker tells court he fired gun." 2008 <http:www.lvrj.com/news> "60 outlaw bikers arrested." Daily News [LA] 22Oct2008: A3.

155 Daily News [LA] 22Oct2008: A3.

156 Daily News [LA] 26Jan2009: A6.

157 "Organized Gangs and Drug Trafficking." 2006 <http://www.usdoj.gov/ndic/pubs11/18862/gangs.htm>

158 "Corruption" <http://www.drugwarfacts.org>

159 "Official Corruption And The War on Drugs The Other Casualty In The War On Drugs: Faith In Law Enforcement." <http://www.csdp.org/news/news/corruption.htm> Lynn, Judi ."U.S. soldier pleads guilty to smuggling drugs from Colombia" <http://www.democraticunderground.com/discuss/duboard.php?az=show_mesg&forum=102&topic_id-1785277&mseg_id=1785277>

160 Ibid

161 "Former Air Force sergeant pleads guilty in border corruption case." 2009. <http://www.latimes.com/news/nationworld/nation/la-na-border-corruption>

162 "Law Enforcement: This Week's Corrupt Cop Stories." 2008. <http://stopthedrugwar.org/565/police_drug_corruption>

163 Official Corruption And The War on Drugs The Other Casualty In The War On Drugs: Faith In Law Enforcement." <http://www.csdp.org/news/news/corruption.htm>

164 "Law Enforcement: This Week's Corrupt Cop Stories" 2009. <http://storthedrugwar.org/chronicle/572/police_drug_corruption."

165 "Crime story: Corrupt cop aided Mexican drug trafficker." 2006 <http:/www.renewamerica.us/columns/kouri/060402>

166 "Cash, cars, jewelry: Some corruption cases involving immigration officers." 2006 <http://USATODAY.com>

167   "Customs and Border Protection officer convicted in drug distribution scheme." 2008 <http://www.usdoj.gov/usao/flw/PressReleases/080201-01.html>

168   "Report to the Chaiman, Permanent Subcommittee on Investigations, Committee on Governmental Affairs, U.S. Senate." 1999 <http://www.gao.gov/archive/2000/rc00003.pdf>

169   "Germans poisoned by lead added to Marijuana." 2008 <http://mjguide.com/modules.php>

170   http://www.streetdrugs.org/marijuana2.htm <http://www.drugs-forum.com/forum/showthread.php>

171   www.thehomegrown.com/articlw/marijuana/beginers2.html "Marijuana prices in the USA.." 2006 <http??www.e-stoned.com/rec/44-Marijuana-Prices-in-the-USA>

172   www.thehomegrown.com/articlw/marijuana/beginers2.html "Marijuana prices in the USA.." 2006 <http??www.e-stoned.com/rec/44-Marijuana-Prices-in-the-USA>

173   "Adulterated Cocaine." 1887 <http://query.nytimes.com/gst/abstract.html>

174   "Tests Show Dealers Adulterating Illegal Drugs." <http://www.redorbit.com/modules/news/tools.php>

175   "Quantitative determination of major cutting agents in cocaine samples seized in Slovenia in the period from May 2004 to November 2005." http://www.tiaft2006.org/proceedings/pdf/DA-p-03/pdf, "Contaminated Cocaine Warning." http://

homelessnation.org/en/node/14387 "Tests Show Dealers Adulterating Illegal Drugs." <http://www.redorbit.com/modules/news/tools.php>

176 "Tests Show Dealers Adulterating Illegal Drugs." http://www.redorbit.com/modules/news/tools.php "Quantitative determination of major cutting agents in cocaine samples seized in Slovenia in the period from May 2004 to November 2005." http://www.tiaft2006.org/proceedings/pdf/DA-p-03/pdf

177 "Adultery for heroin users." 2008 http://www.mindhacks.com/blog/2008/11/adultery_for_heroin_.html "Fentanl-laced Heroin Kills Hundreds Of Addicts in USA." 2006 <http://www.medicalnewstoday.com/printerfriendlynews.php>

178 Tests Show Dealers Adulterating Illegal Drugs." http://www.redorbit.com/modules/news/tools.php, "Fact Sheet Heroin" http://lxion.demon.co.uk/heroin.htm, "Stronger heroin suspected in overdose spicks." <http://www.news.com.au/perthnow/story.o,27574,25151668-2761,00.htm>

179 "United Nations Office on Drugs and Crime 2007", http://www.unodc.org/pdf/research/wdro7/wdr, "Illegal Drugs and Drug Trafficking" <http://www.parl.gc.ca/information/library/PRBpubs/bp435-3htm>

180 "Illegal Drugs and Drug Trafficking" <http: //www.parl.gc.ca/information/library/PRBpubs/bp435-3htm>"Illicit Finance", 2008 <http://www.usdoj.gov/ndic/pubs31/31379/finance.htm>

181 "State Sales Tax Rates" <http://www.taxadmin.org/FTA/rate/sales.html>

182 "State Liquor Excise Tax Rates" http://www.taxadmin.org/fta/rate/liquor.html, http://www.bevmo.com/Shop/ProductList.aspx>, http://www.bevmo.com/Wine.aspx, "State Excise Tax Rates on Cigarettes", 2008, http://www.taxadmin.org/fla/rate/cigarett.html, <http://www.cigarettepricesearch.com/cigarette-cheapest-prices/winston.htm>, http://www.cigarettepricesearch.com/cigarette-cheapest-prices/camel.htm, <http://www.cigarettepricesearch.com/cigarette-cheapest-prices/marlboro.htm>

183 <http://by129w.bay129.mail.live.com/mail/PrintShell.aspx>

184 "Corporate and Individual Tax Data", <http:www.smbiz.com/sbr1001.html>

185 "USDOJ: About DOJ - Alphabetical List of Agencies", <http://www.usdoj.gov/02organizations/02_1.html>

186 "DEA Staffing and Budget", <http://www.usdoj.gov/dea/agency/staffing.htm> , "Stats & Facts", <http://www.usdoj.gov/dea/statistics.html>

187 <http://www.usnews.com/articles/opinion/2008/12/31> <http://www.city-data.com/forum/california/> "Summary of Proposed 2009 Appropriations by funds, Departments, and Object Classifications - Continued"<http://egov.cityofchicago.org/webportal/cocw> <http://dallascithhall.com/human_resources/index.html> <http://www.lapdonline.org/lapd_command_staff/comm_bio_view/7603> <http://www.nyc.gov/html/census/popcur.shtml>

188 <http://www.justice.gov/jmd/2008summary/ pdf/004_budget_highlights.pdf>, DrugWarFacts. org "Prison & Drug Offenders <http://www. drugwarfacts.org/cms/node/63>

189 <http://www.drugwarfacts.org/cms/ node/63>,Riordan, Jessica "More than One in 100 Adults are Behind Bars" <http://www. pewcenteronthestates.org/news_room_detail. aspx>

190 Daily News [LA] 05Dec2008 :A3; Daily News [LA] 10Feb20097 :A5

191 Daily News [LA] 17Mar2009 : A4 Daily News [LA] 05Aug2009 :A1

192 <http://www.pewcenteronthestates.org/news_ room_detail.aspx><http://www.whitehouse.gov/ omb/rewrite/budget/fy2007/justice.html>

193 <http://www.dhs.gov/xlibrary/assets/budget_ bibfy2008.pdf>, http://www.dhs.gov/xabout/ history/>, http://www.dhs.gov/xlibrary/phoots/ orgchart-web.png>

194 <http://www.cbp.gov>

195 ibid

196 ibid

197 <http://www.uscg.mil/posturestatement/?topPage =budgetinbrief&subPage=table 2>, <http://www. uscg.mil/hq/cg5/cg531/drug_interdiction.asp>, <http://www.uscg.mil/hq/cg5/cg531/Drugs/stats. asp>

198   Senate Bill 1070. 2010 <http://www.azleg.gov/legtext/49leg/2r/bills/sb1070.s.pdf>

199   "Pinal Sheriff: Smugglers probably killed 2 men in desert" 11 Jun 2010< http://www.abc15.com/dpp/news/region_central_southern_az/other/pinal-sheriff%3A-smugglers-probably-killed-2-men-in-desert.>"Kidnappings, Home Invasions Sparked Ariz. law" 27 Apr 2010<http://www.newsmax.com/US/immigration-arizona-crime-kidnappings/2010/04/27/13/357099>

200   "Phoenix, as kidnapping capital, sees drop in abductions" 28 Dec 2009<http.www.kvoa.com/news/phoenix-as-kidnapping-capital-sees-drop-in-dbductions/>

201   11 Jun. 2010< http://www.azcentral.com/business/articles/2010/05/13/20100513immigration-boycotts-list.html>, "Immigration law supporters rally in Arizona" 5 Jun 2010<http://latimesblogs.latimes.com/dcnow/2010/06/immigration-law-supporters-rally-in-arizona.html>"Poizner Voices Support For Arizona Immigration Law" 2 May 2010<http://cbs5.com/local/steve.poizner.voices.2.1670262.html><Martin, Jonathan "2010 Complete Election Coverage: GOP could gain by raising Arizona" 5 May 2010 <http://www.politico.com/news/stories/0510/36790.html>Bown, Alison "Thousands Rally in Support of Comprehensive Immigration Reform: Against Arizona Law." 3 May 2010<http://latindispatch.com/2010/05/03/thousands-rally-in-support-of-comprehensive-immigration-reform-against-arizona-law/Archibold, Randal C. "Arizona

Enacts Stringent Law on Immigration." 23 Apr 2010<http://www.nytimes.com/2010/04/24/us/politics/24immig.html>< Barry, Sean." Tourism backlash over immigration law could cost Arizona bond rating, tens of millions" 11 May,.2010:<http://rawstory.com/rs/2010/0511/arizona-law-threatens-states-bond-rating/>

202 Dolin, Benjamin. "National Drug Policy: The Netherlands" 15 August 2001 <http://www.parl.gc.ca/37/1/parlbus/commbus/senate/Com-e/ille-e/library-e/dolin1-e.htm>

203 <http://www.amsterdam.info/coffeshops>;<http://www.drugwarfacts.org/cms/node/67>

204 DrugWarFacts.org "The Netherlands Compared With the United States" <http://www.drugwarfacts.org/cms/node/67>

205 <http://vote96.sos.ca.gov/bp/215text.htm>

206 <http://www.tokeofthetown.com/2010/04/ la_city_council_approves_pot_dispensary_fee_schedu.php><http://www.ocnoml.org/medical/southern_california_dspensaries.htm<>laounty.gov>

207 <http://www.tokeofthetown.com/2010/04/la_city_council_approves_pot_dispensary_fee_schedu.php><http://www.ocnornl.org/medical/southern_california_dispensaries.htm><lacounty.gov>

208 <http://ag.ca.gov/crime.php>< http://ag.ca.gov/cjsc/glance/cht2.php>